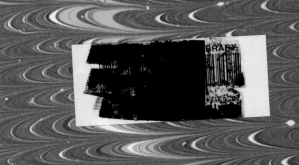

Dedication

For Ramón, Ravi, Shirley,
and in memory of Herman.

Designed by Bonnie Hensley

Printed in the United States of America.
ISBN: 0-88740-548-7

Published by Schiffer Publishing, Ltd.
77 Lower Valley Road
Atglen, PA 19310
Please write for a free catalog.
This book may be purchased from the publisher.
Please include $2.95 postage.
Try your bookstore first.

We are interested in hearing from authors
with book ideas on related subjects.

Credits

Collecting is a peculiar concept. The treasure-hunt posture of the search and the private thrill of the find can be more compelling than the apparent goal of displaying or using the collection. Possession is not an end, because it motivates a quest for similar objects and for information about them. There is a natural curiosity to learn more about objects already in ones possession, so some of the best sources of information about art are the private collectors, as well as the public collectors, or museums. My thanks to those private collectors who generously lent glass to be photographed for this book: Dr. Albert and Marilyn Bennett, George and Lois Epstein, Shirley Friedland, Merv and Silvia Glickman, Michael Joseph, Robert Josephson, Ralph and Terry Kovel, Mort and Mal Peck, Valerie Pollak, Anita Singer, and many others who wish to remain anonymous.

The two major international auction houses, Sotheby's and Christie's, must be credited with providing information, setting standards, and establishing a market in fifties glass. Their auction catalogs become reference books, and I am grateful for the use of photographs from these catalogs: Sotheby's Geneva *Venetian Glass 1910-1960* (Nov. 10, 1990), Christie's London *Modern Glass and Ceramics* (June 23, 1987), and Christie's New York *Property from the Estate of Robert Mapplethorpe* (Oct. 31, 1989).

Dr. Angelo Barovier generously lent photos of Barovier & Toso glass from the catalog *Ercole Barovier 1889-1974* and supplied information. Thanks to another great glassworks, Orrefors, which provided and permitted me to reprint some of the beautiful photos from the *Orrefors Gallery 1984/85* as well as material on signatures and dating. I would like to thank Franklin and Ramona Knower for permission to reprint pages from their book, *Erickson Freehand Glass.* Among the best sources for contemporary photos of high style design is the Italian monthly review of architecture, interiors, and art, *Domus,* and I am grateful for permission to use some of these 50s photographs.

Brunschwig and Fils and groundworks unlimited, both at the Ohio Design Centre in Beachwood, Ohio supplied backdrops for some photos, and others were provided by Shirley Friedland. A very special thanks to Hank Schulte, who generously and repeatedly lent us camera equipment, and it worked rather well when we finally learned how to use it. To my son Ravi who sacraficed his valuable teenage time to shoot all of the photos not credited otherwise, (not to mention the use of his Macintosh) thank you. And thanks, Ramón, for taking the measurements and for overlooking the mess in the house.

Without libraries and their staffs, little research could be done, and I would like to thank the Corning Museum of Glass Library for being a genuinely user-friendly library as well as a wonderful resource, Cleveland Public Library, Cleveland Museum of Art Library, Cleveland Institute of Art Library, the use of Ralph and Terry Kovel's personal library, and the Ursuline College Library. Since some books were in languages other than English, thanks to my colleague at Ursuline, Olga Lombardi, for Italian translations. Another colleague and lifelong friend, Paula Bloch, proofread the manuscript, and any remaining errors are mine. Of course none of these thanks would be needed if Nancy Schiffer did not encourage me from the start. Schiffer Publishing, with its fine editorial staff, is a writer's dream for friendly personalized support and guidance.

Introduction

The 1950s were memorable years for design, notably in the decorative or applied arts. Vibrant often flamboyant color, slick smooth surfaces, and novel forms such as biomorphic blobs (asymmetrical organic shapes like those seen in sculpture by Jean Arp or paintings by Salvador Dali) and stretched amoeboid shapes were found on anything from cocktail tables to the glass ashtrays on top of them. Designers had fresh ideas for the whimsical and the sophisticated, yet there was an unmistakable continuity of style and coordination among diverse art forms.

Naturally, none of this occurred in historic isolation. Modernism had been evolving for decades with the Wiener Werkstätte, European Art Moderne in the 1920s, American Deco in the 1930s, the International Style, and the Bauhaus. Similarities between early Modernist and fifties designs are apparent in furniture, metal, ceramics, textiles, and graphics, but with few exceptions one art form stands out from what had been done before —glass. Fifties glass was different. During the span of a few years, glass artists achieved unprecedented success with innovative design and exhibited awesome technical virtuosity. That is not to say that fifties glass was more important than other media, but collectively it created a look that could represent the design of a decade.

The term "fifties glass" does not refer to all glass made in the 1950s because much (if not most) was neither new nor representative of the modern aesthetic of those years. Many companies continued to produce glass in earlier styles that had been shown repeatedly over past decades or centuries. Nor are mass-produced utilitarian wares and architectural glass included in this volume. Fifties glass is only the artistic or "designer" glass made by individuals or, more often, teams working in studio departments of large glass factories or in glass factories organized in a similar manner. The decade of the 1950s, wedged between the postwar years and the beginning of the studio glass movement of the 1960s, witnessed an explosion of creative activity inspired by individual designers employed by large firms.

Many glassmaking centers participated in this exciting event, but two geographic areas outshine the others in innovation, quality, and productivity —Italy and Scandinavia. Italy, specifically the island of Murano off the coast of Venice, has been either the Western world's premier glassmaking center or a major hub for the past 500 years. Renaissance Venetian glass was so highly prized that its technical secrets could be compared to modern day classified military or scientific information. Though its makers were accorded high status, they were kept captive on the island of Murano to prevent the glass secrets from leaking out. Inevitably, some Venetian glassmakers found their way to other European countries, hence, the term "façon de Venice," or "in the Venetian fashion." After a long decline, glassmaking was revived in Murano in the nineteenth century, but it was not until the 1920s that modern styles began to be developed. The culmination of the long history of technical achievement, plus the modern design ideas of the 1950s, once again placed Murano at center stage in the art of glassmaking.

Scandinavian glass had a much different history, partly because its geographic range included several large countries, each with a separate course of events. Yet fifties glass at Orrefors, Kosta, and other Swedish companies, and in Finland, Denmark, and Norway, shared some obvious characteristics with each other and, more subtly, with Murano. Scandinavian glass artists did not use color as it was used in Murano; theirs was cooler, more transparent, and rarely as vibrant. Clear glass also continued to be made, though some had inclusions of color. Forms were sometimes similar to those in Murano; thick-walled glass with internal decoration replaced the characteristically cool Northern etching or engraving of surfaces. Innovations included techniques such as Ariel, Graal, and Ravenna, which relied on multi-layered glass with both controlled and spontaneous abstract designs. Here the glass medium emulated the fine art of painting. Meanwhile in Murano, abstraction was also incorporated into glass design, thereby expanding the repertoire of stripes and filigree to include patchwork and asymmetrical painting in glass. Fifties artists had broken loose from previous constraints of the medium.

Companies such as Venini, Barovier & Toso, Kosta, and Orrefors were leaders because of their consistency in quality, desire for innovation, and sheer volume of production. Other companies paralleled the stars of Murano and Scandinavia by sharing similar ideas and even some of their designers. Murano glass, the most dramatically varied in both design and technique, is better represented than Scandinavian in the following chapters, though the quality is comparable. What gave fifties glass its "look" simply occurred more in Murano than anywhere else. It is no surprise that Italy dominated the art glass industry during the decade of the 50s; after all, Venice enjoyed a dominant position throughout the Renaissance and continued to play an important, though uneven, role for three more centuries. What is puzzling is that other countries that had previously made significant artistic contributions in glass, including Czechoslovakia, England, France, and the United States, were not also leaders in the 50s. Industrial production of everything from containers to architectural glass was strong in England and the United States, but hand made art glass production was meager. Exceptions such as Blenko and Erickson glass are included here because, although these American companies may not have shared the quality of design and technique with Murano furnaces, the spirit of the fifties did touch them. This American mold-blown tableware displayed the vibrant color, the shapes, and some of the internal decoration that gave mainstream fifties glass its distinctiveness. High quality clear crystal was the only product made by Daum and Steuben, companies that had been in the spotlight a few decades earlier for their colorful art glass. Now at the conservative end of fifties glass activity, only the shapes were new. Artists in Czechoslovakia were quietly doing some good designing, but outside of World Fairs, word did not often reach Western Europe.

As with any complicated phenomenon, there are complicated reasons for the rise or decline of glass industries on a national scale. In my opinion, personalities, individual stars, were more essential than one might imagine. Take, for example, Louis Comfort Tiffany (1848-1933), today a household word and a name synonymous with American Art Nouveau glass (as well as generic replicas). The fact that Tiffany was more a manager than a glass artist is ironic but, nevertheless, irrelevant. His prodigious operation in Corona, New York gave the United States its only position in the Art Nouveau movement. But for those short years, the United States was not a country renowned for art glass. In fact, America's contribution was typically not one of art but of industry and mechanization with the development (if not invention) of pressed glass —the democratization of an art form through a means of mass-production. Pressed and molded glass were America's mainstay. Brilliant cut lead crystal toward the end of the nineteenth century was another American contribution. Then Tiffany arrived via interior decorating and orchestrated an art glass bonanza. There were others, notably Frederick Carder (1863-1963), who began his career in England but emigrated to America and founded Steuben Glassworks. Carder was a prolific and extraordinarily gifted glass designer and craftsman but today is less known than Tiffany. Similarly, in France during the Art Nouveau period, the name Emile Gallé (1846-1904) became equated with French cameo glass. There were, of course, other personalities, the Daum brothers (Auguste 1853-1909 and Antonin 1864-1930) for instance, but none as great or influential as Gallé.

What I am suggesting is that these individual superstars, for whatever complex reasons, were not just part of the history of the medium. They were that history, if only for a moment. This may sound recklessly oversimplified and exaggerated, but then history does have a tendancy to appear that way. If the names Tiffany and Carder were synonymous with American Art Nouveau glass, and if Gallé followed by Daum and others were the French stars, when their careers or lives ended, so did the moment. France was coincidentally the place of origin for Art Deco as well as Art Nouveau, and in the category of glass, another giant, René Lalique (1860-1945), monopolized the Art Deco niche. Ironically, his luxury glass was molded and commercially produced rather than blown (techniques which had been something of a disqualifying factor for the United States). As in the case of Tiffany, a man of artistic vision and managerial genius (who hardly held a blowpipe), what matters about Lalique is his role in establishing France at the front of the Art Deco glass scene.

The French people at the turn of the century were not involved in the glass industry any more than the population of fifteenth-century Italy. Remarkably talented individuals were rare, but there were enough of them to have done all of the glassmaking. We probably do not see much bad Renaissance glass today, because people have not been inclined to save bad art over the years. The point is that once the social, political, and economic backgrounds were in place, unless these rare individual personalities appeared, none of the art from the Italian Renaissance to the French Art Nouveau period could develop. Whether it be Thomas Chippendale obviously synthesizing Gothic, Rococo, and Chinese styles, Frank Lloyd Wright subtly incorporating East into West to produce something rather original (there is no such thing as totally original), or Angelo Barovier perfecting cristallo in quatrocento Murano, the great names are what make styles and chapters in history books.

Therefore, one explanation for the dominance of Italy and Scandinavia in the fifties glass arena is a simple one: personalities such as Venini, Barovier, Seguso, Wirkkala, Sarpeneva, Lindstrand, and others happened to appear at about the same time and in the same place (or places). With that amount of energy and talent plus a nurturing environment, the fifties phenomenon was practically unavoidable. A comparable group of individuals did not appear in other countries at that time, or if any did appear, the context was not suitable, which might explain why other countries produced little if any fifties glass.

Pieces from France, the Netherlands, the United States, etc. are, however, included in a chapter called "other countries," because good glass was produced that falls within the focus of this book. As collectors, dealers, curators, and historians research and share their discoveries in this relatively new area, more

countries and artists will surely surface. I have attempted to show a representative sample of the many wonderful objects called fifties glass, from the relatively common to the unusual or perhaps unique. A range exists in both quality and value. Although designer pieces are stressed, examples from anonymously made tourist items to museum quality art share the label fifties glass. The categories of illustrations are not arranged conventionally by artists, companies, or even by countries in any systematic way. Rather, as an aid to collectors, they are grouped according to visual characteristics. For example, if a collector wishes to identify a piece of striped glass, which could have been made by one of several Muranese artists and companies, the section on stripes should be an easy reference. Unfortunately, many pieces are unsigned, sometimes because an original paper label has been lost. As more signed or attributed pieces become known, these will help to identify other pieces by comparison.

As I tell my students—if you go away from this class with no more than an appreciation for the objects we have looked at together, then I am satisfied. If you have enjoyed the experience and gained a respect for the designers and artisans who have provided it, then the class was a success. The intent of this book is the same—in this case, to whet the appetite for a colorful and special moment in the history of decorative art.

Contents

CHAPTER I

Italy

In *Modern Glass*, published in 1962, Ada Polak wrote that the Venini firm was still the leading glassmaker in Murano. Decades later the statement can still be made, although some would argue that the 50s were really the best years because Paulo Venini (died 1959) was the most creative force of the company. Some of the 50s designs by Carlo Scarpa, Fulvio Bianconi, and Venini actually date back to the 1940s, but greater production and recognition at international exhibitions occurred during the 1950s. In addition to Venini, other Muranese superstars, Alfredo Barbini, Ercole Barovier, Gino Cenedese, Antonio Salviati, and Archimede Seguso, created such momentum in the 50s that their glass factories are among the leaders in Murano today. Their earlier production is also gaining well-deserved recognition.

Although fifties designs by Venini and others were modern, they were not done without reference to the history of Venetian glassmaking. If one technique can characterize that history, it would be latticino, the use of fine threadlike and thicker strands of filigree internally decorating the otherwise clear cristallo. Similarly, if one technique or set of techniques could characterize the Venini factory it would also be filigree, especially the zanfirico, or twisted filigree patterns. Venini's designers and master glassblowers took the glass thread and colored, twisted, and wove it as it had never been done before.

Vetro filigrana *Photo courtesy of ©Domus (314:48, Jan. 1956)*

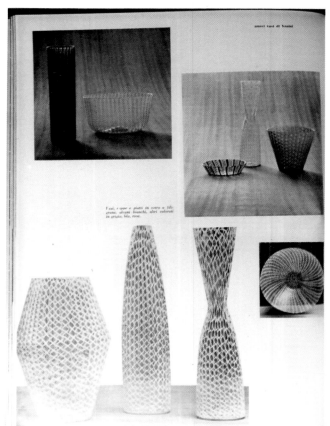

Venini vetro filigrana *Photo courtesy of ©Domus (361:38, Dec. 1959)*

Venini vetro filigrana *Photo courtesy of ©Domus (361:38/39 insert, Dec. 1959)*

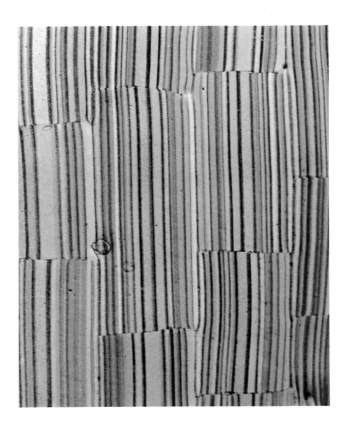

Mosaic glass by Venini *Photo courtesy of ©Domus (333:47, Aug. 1957)*

Domus cover with Venini mosaic glass *Photo courtesy of ©Domus (333:cover, Aug. 1957)*

Murano is a small island with glassmaking its focus. If a technique for forming, coloring or decorating glass is introduced by a glass artist at one company, it is likely that someone at another company will hear about it, explore its possibilities, develop it further, and then incorporate his individual style. Zanfirico was used in one form or another by most Murano glassmakers, and in addition to Venini, zanfirico masterpieces of technical virtuousity and artistic merit were made by Archimede Seguso, Barovier & Toso, Aureliano Toso, and others. These and other glass factories used a modern variation of another Italian Renaissance glassmaking technique, using slices of multicolored canes and patches of colored glass in mosaic designs (actually an ancient Roman innovation predating the Renaissance by about 1500 years). For mosaic or murrhine glass, the firm of Barovier & Toso is best known for successfully introducing both imaginative designs and masterful techniques. And like the popular filigree, murrhine glass was also made by other firms, including Venini.

Another decorative technique that gives Venetian glass its distinctive look is the use of metallic particles and powders. These can be controlled within the glass by first mixing the metal with liquid cristallo (clear glass) and using it in stripes and patches, a technique which is called aventurine. Another method involves taking thin sheets of gold or silver leaf, applying them to the surface of the hot glass, then blowing the vessel. As the hot vessel expands, the thin metal on the surface breaks apart, leaving tiny patches or particles. Aside from the company's early years, Venini did not usually use metal particles as decoration. Other important furnaces such as Archimede Seguso, Barovier & Toso, and Barbini achieved some intriguing effects with metallic inclusions.

Murano glass *Photo courtesy of ©Domus (298:52, Sept. 1954)*

One technique in particular that gives glass from both Italy and Sweden a distinctive fifties look can also make attribution of unmarked pieces confusing. Sommerso, or colored shapes encased in very thick glass, was used successfully in both countries. Flavio Poli designed them for Seguso Vetri d'Arte in Murano, while Vicke Lindstrand worked for Kosta in Sweden, and other companies made similar versions. They each designed forms based on the water droplet with thick clear or colored transparent

glass encasing a shape of another color. These heavy sculptural vessels seemed to make the transition between decorative or applied art with a function and fine art without. Eventually, the opening was omitted, the implied function of a vase or other vessel was unnecessary, and art glass took the step to glass art.

The objects in this chapter depict the styles and techniques used by companies in Murano during the 1950s. Some were, in fact, designed or executed slightly earlier or later, but, nevertheless, also help to define the category called fifties glass. Pieces are arranged, though sometimes loosely, by visual qualities resulting from specific glassmaking techniques, rather than by artists or companies. For each technique presented, there are undoubtedly other variations not shown; there are also the designs developed especially for one of the international exhibitions, and examples may be rare. The fact is there will always be more works of art excluded from books than those pictured. I have attempted to portray fifties Murano glass in this chapter as a varied and wildly colorful art form that took its inspiration from the past, developed a new look during what may have been the most significant single decade in the history of glassmaking, and has continued to inspire glassmakers ever since.

All objects are in private collections unless otherwise stated. Sizes are approximate.

Venini vases in series "Pennellate," "Spicchi," and "Pezzuto" *Photo courtesy of ©Domus (361:42, Dec. 1959)*

1.1 A.V.E.M. vase in zanfirico and millefiori Asymmetrical vase with wide bent neck and hole piercing the body in polychrome patchwork of zanfirico canes and millefiori cane sections. H. 15 in. (38 cm.) unsigned. *Photo courtesy of Sotheby's*

1.2 left **Venini mezza filigrana vase, and filigrana plate attributed to Venini** Flared cylindrical vase in clear glass internally decorated with thin white diagonal lines, or mezza filigrana. H. 9¾ in. (24.5 cm.) paper label VENINI MURANO The plate of clear glass decorated with fine white threads, the rim highlighted with turquoise. D. 8⅝ in. (22 cm.) unsigned

back center and right **Mezza filigrana vase and bowl attributed to Venini** Flared cylindrical vase of clear glass internally decorated in pale green and white mezza filigrana. H. 15¾ in. (40 cm.) unsigned Circular flared bowl of clear glass internally decorated with pale green mezza filigrana. D. 8 in. (20 cm.) unsigned

front center **Venini filigrana leaf-shaped dish by Tyra Lundgreen** The dish with an irregularly folded rim in clear glass with opaque pale blue-green lines. L. 9½ in. (24 cm.) acid stamp VENINI MURANO ITALIA

right **Filigrana a reticello bowl attributed to Venini** Flared circular bowl of clear glass internally decorated with amethyst weaving and externally with white, intersecting and forming a network of diamond shapes with an air bubble in each. H. 3½ in. (9 cm.) unsigned. *Photo Courtesy of Christie's*

1.3 **Zanfirico plates** These two nearly identical clear glass plates have intricate patterns of twisted filigree radiating from the center, each with white zanfirico alternating with white and gold metallic zanfirico, one plate with yellow-green. These may have been made by Venini, as both the styles and fineness of the filigree are characteristic of that firm. D. 7½ in. (18.4 cm.) unsigned

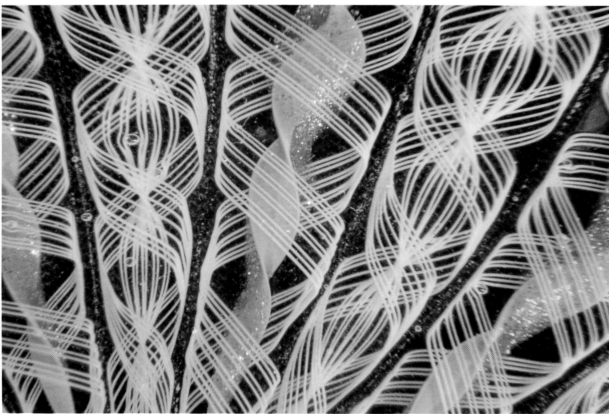

1.4 **Zanfirico detail**

1.5 Zanfirico vase Tapered vase with applied opaque black base and black stripes alternating with clear canes with extremely fine yellow threading in spiral zanfirico, possibly by Venini. H 8½ in. (21.6 cm.) unsigned

1.6 **Detail of black and yellow zanfirico** Other than Venini or Archimede Seguso, few companies produced any filigree this fine.

1.7 Miniature zanfirico cups Three small cups in zanfirico: left in green, copper metallic, and white; center copper metallic and white; right in pink, green, copper metallic, and bluish-purple. H. 1⅝ in. (4.1 cm.) unsigned

1.8 Detail of miniature cup

1.9 **Reticello ramekins** Ruffled bowls with saucers of clear glass with internal gold metallic stripes crossing diagonally with external lattimo threading, an air bubble trapped in the diamond shape created by the intersecting stripes, possibly by Venini. bowl H. 2½ in. (6.3 cm) saucer D. 4½ in. (11.4 cm.) unsigned

1.10 **Reticello detail**

1.11 **Venini filigree bowl** Bowl of clear glass canes with white filigree alternating with turquoise filigree in spiral stripes radiating from the center. D. 4⅜ in (11.1 cm) acid stamp VENINI MURANO ITALIA

1.12 **Detail of Venini filigree**

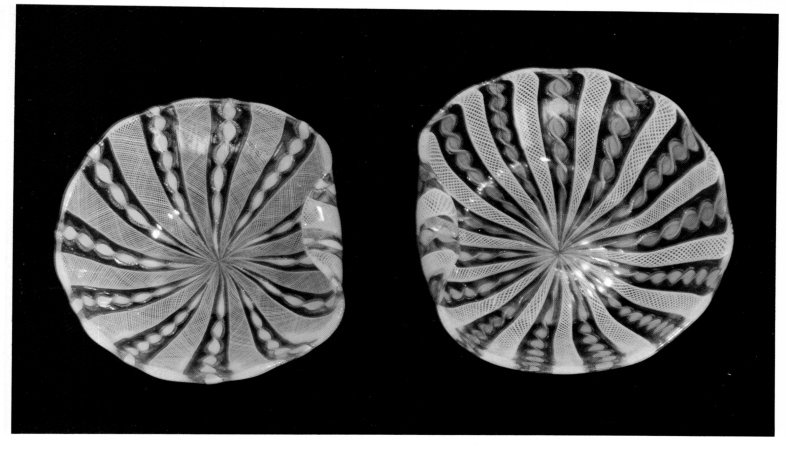

1.13 Zanfirico bowls Canes of clear glass and white netted zanfirico alternating with either yellow or pink twisted ribbons with gold metallic powder, the stripes radiating from the center, and each bowl with a folded edge. pink D. 5⅛ in. (13 cm.) unsigned

1.14 Folded zanfirico bowls Set of four bowls with blue and metallic gold ribbons alternating with white netted zanfirico, the sides pinched and folded, (a reminder that the glass was once hot and liquid, so typical of fifties shapes.) average D. 4 in. (10.2 cm.) unsigned

1.15 **Zanfirico bowl with stretched appendages** Heavy clear glass bowl or ashtray with stripes of white netting, copper metallic powders, and brown twisted filigree radiating from the center, the ends pulled out to create another fifties biomorphic shape. D. 10 in. (25.4 cm.) unsigned

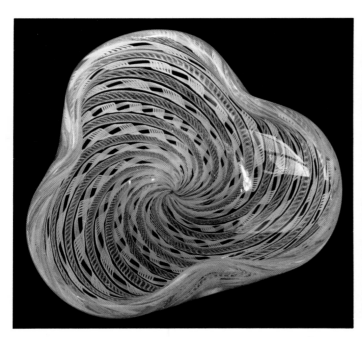

1.16 **Zanfirico trefoil bowl** Thick clear glass internally decorated with finely executed stripes of white and aventurine in an alternating twisted filigree pattern spiraling from the center, in the form of a trefoil shaped bowl. D. 7½ in. (19.1 cm) unsigned

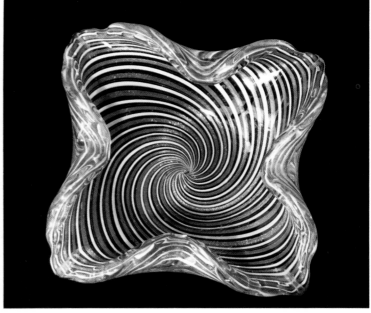

1.17 **Spiral striped quatrafoil bowl** Alternating lattimo and aventurine stripes spiraling from the center of a quatrafoil shaped bowl with sides folded inward. D. 9 in. (22.9 cm.) unsigned

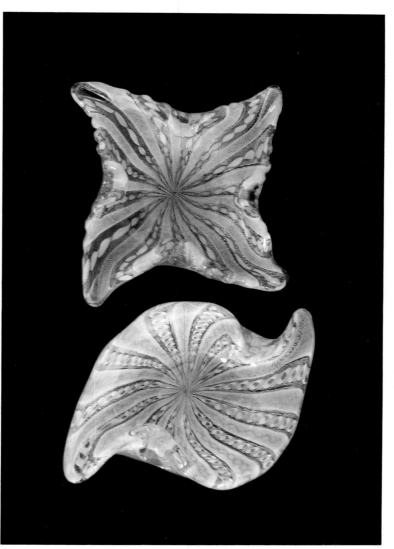

1.19 **Zanfirico leaf bowls** Three clear glass bowls in the form of leaves, each with stripes of white netting alternating with either yellow-green, blue, or copper metallic stripes radiating from the center. average L. 5 in. (12.7 cm.) unsigned

1.18 **Two zanfirico bowls in biomorphic shapes** Two heavy clear glass bowls or ashtrays, each of white netted filigree stripes alternating with pink and copper metallic ribbons radiating from the center, the one with two stretched appendages and the other with four, the shapes resembling sea creatures. top D. 11⅛ in. (28.3 cm) bottom D. 12 in. (30.5 cm.) unsigned

1.20 **Three small folded bowls** left, in multicolored canes radiating from the center with two edges folded over; center, with turquoise and clear glass alternating stripes radiating from the center overlaid with lattimo thread radiating in the opposite direction, the edge in a toothlike pattern; right, in white filigree netting alternating with orange twisted filigree and three edges folded inward. average D. 4⅝ in. (11.8 cm.) unsigned

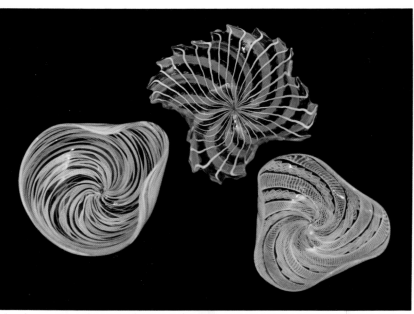

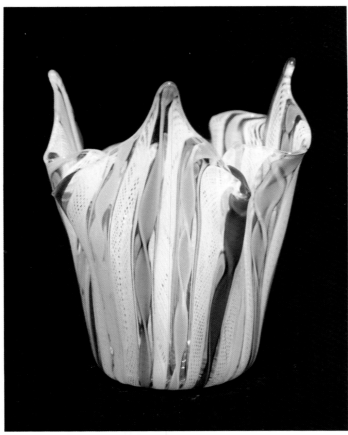

1.21 **Fazzoletto vase** Handkerchief-shaped vase in popular zanfirico pattern of white netting alternating with multi-colored ribbons. H. 5¼ in. (13.3 cm.) unsigned

1.23 **Zanfirico carafe** Pastel colored ribbons alternating with white netted stripes in the form of a caraffe with stopper of identical zanfirico pattern and applied handle of clear glass with copper metallic inclusions. H. 11 in. (28 cm.) unsigned

1.22 **Large zanfirico vase with clear foot** Large footed vase in popular zanfirico stripes of white netted pattern alternating with colored ribbons of pink, blue, green, and yellow, on a foot of clear glass with copper metallic inclusions. H. 15 in. (38.1 cm.) unsigned

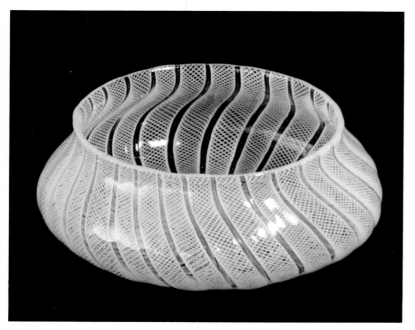

1.24 **White latticino bowl** Flattened bulbous bowl tapered to a narrower rim, the clear glass internally decorated with lattimo filigree. D. 5½ in. (14 cm.) unsigned

1.25 **Three zanfirico bells** Each glass bell of clear glass internally decorated in parallel stripes of netted and twisted filigree: pink and white, white, and yellow and white. tallest H. 5¼ in. (13.3 cm.)

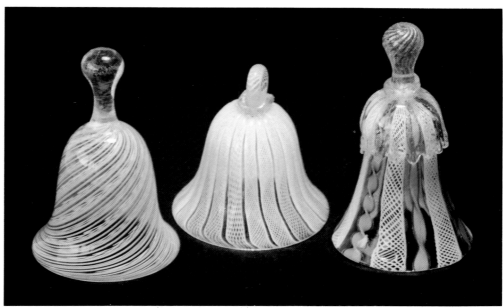

1.26 **Zanfirico bowl with saucer** Stripes of clear glass internally decorated with white netting alternating with green ribbon and metallic powder, all radiating from the center of the bowl and saucer. bowl D. 4⅝ in. (12.1 cm.) saucer D. 7⅝ in. (19.4 cm.) unsigned, although a very similar example illustrated in Dorigato (1983, p. 68) is by Salviati.

1.29 **Filigrana miniature cup and saucer attributed to Seguso Vetri d'Arte, designed by Flavio Poli** Fine lattimo filigree with intermittant green threading in the clear glass, the handleless cup in parallel and diagonal mezza filigrana, the saucer with striping spiraling from the center, and the base and rims in candy-striped green and white twist. H. 1½ in. (3.8 cm.) saucer D. 3⅜ in. (8,6 cm.) unsigned, although an almost identical example by Flavio Poli is illustrated in Aloi (pp. 10 & 11)

1.27 **Filigrana a retortoli vase** Pinched vase of fine lattimo threads twisted around clear canes alternating with copper metallic, pale blue, and white netting, probably by Venini, since this type of complex zanfirico was one of the techniques popularized by the firm. H. 3⅝ in. (9.2 cm.) unsigned

1.28 **Filigrana a retortoli vase** Globular vase with narrow neck and flared lip in pale blue glass stripes alternating with red and white twisted filigree in a diagonal pattern. H. 3⅛ in. (8.3 cm.) unsigned

1.30 **Mezza filigrana vase** Bulbous vase with narrow neck and applied foot of clear glass, the parallel diagonal stripes of lattimo and robin's-egg-blue applied to the surface instead of the usual internal decoration. H. 5⅝ in. (14.3 cm.) unsigned but a vase in the same technique and color (Treadway Nov. 1992 lot no. 160) was designed by Tommaso Buzzi for Venini. *Collection of Lois and George Epstein*

1.31 **Merletto bowl** Amber glass internally decorated with fine lattimo netted pattern in the form of an asymmetrical bowl with rolled end. D. 5¼ in. (13.3 cm.) unsigned but probably by Archimede Seguso, whose series of lace and net patterns are among the most varied and intricate. Closely resembles Harrtil glass from Czechoslovakia. (Glass Collector's Digest Feb/March, 1993 pp. 39-42.)

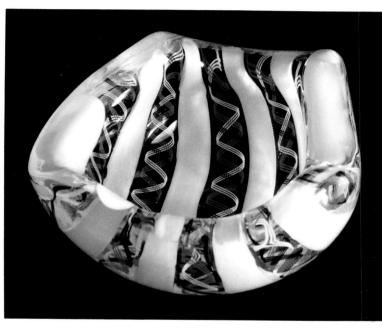

1.33 **Filigrana a retortoli bowl** Thick glass with stripes of wide lattimo canes alternating with clear canes wrapped with fine twisted filigree of black and red-orange, the heavy sculptural form typical of the fifties. D. 4 in. (10.2 cm.) unsigned

1.32 **Merletto bowl** Thick clear glass bowl internally decorated with extremely fine lattimo threads in a lacey or netlike pattern, with clear rim. L. 6¾ in. (17.2 cm.) unsigned but probably by Archimede Seguso unless by Harrtil of Czechoslovakia.

1.34 **Latticino shoe** Clear glass with stripes of white latticino netting alternating with twisted blue ribbon (zanfirico). L. 5¾ in. (14.6 cm.) unsigned

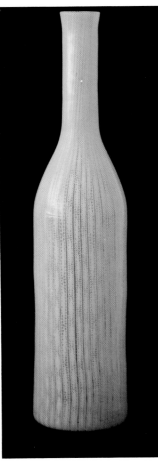

1.36 **Fratelli Toso tall zanfirico bottle** Clear glass bottle with applied exterior parallel vertical stripes of yellow and white zanfirico. H. 15¼ in. (38.7 cm.) paper label: MADE IN ITALY MURANO GLASS identified as Fratelli Toso label (Treadway lot no. 232)

1.35 **Two latticino vases** Double gourd shaped vase of clear glass decorated with pink and white latticino, and a bulbous vase with turquoise and white latticino and applied clear handles. average H. 4 in. (10.2 cm.)

1.37 Scalloped bowl with filigrano a retortoli Thick-walled glass bowl with stripes radiating from the center in opaque black alternating with lattimo twisted filigree. D. 7 in. (17.8 cm.) unsigned

1.38 Venini fazzoletto vase Handkerchief-shaped vase with stripes of transparent purple alternating with fine lattimo netting. H. 3¾ in. (9.5 cm.) D. 4⅞ in. (12.4 cm.) unsigned, though an almost identical example is illustrated in Neuwirth (p. 75) with only a paper Venini label, indicating that this one once had a paper label as well.

1.39 Venini merletto vase designed by Paolo Venini 1954-56 Mold-blown vase with central ovoid body internally decorated in lattimo merletto, or lacework. H. 9⅞ in. (25 cm.) *Photo courtesy of Sotheby's*

1.40 Venini "Vetro Tessuto" vase designed by Carlo Scarpa Squared body ending with a squared neck with narrow vertical stripes in turquoise and amethyst on one side, and turquoise and white on the other. "Vetro Tessuto," also known as cloth glass or fabric glass, was named by Venini. The division of the stripes into two distinct areas was considered a radical design in its day and is one of Scarpa's most celebrated models. H. 7½ in. (19 cm.) acid stamp VENINI MURANO ITALIA *Photo courtesy of Christie's*

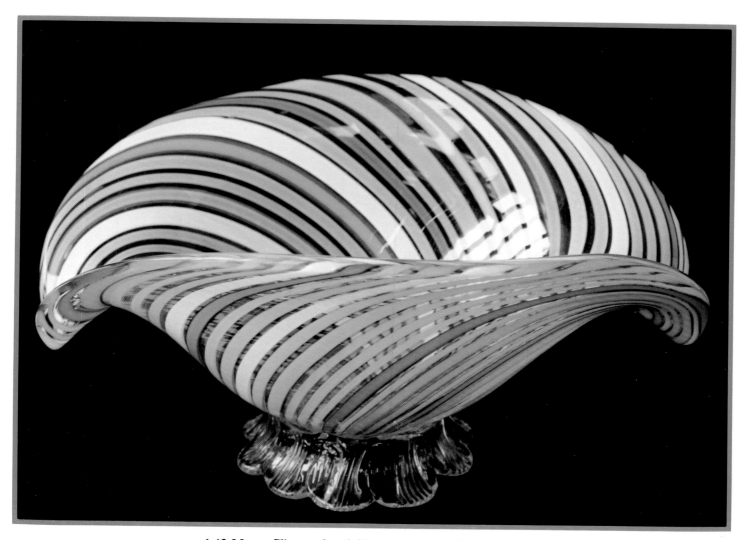

1.42 **Mezza filigrana bowl** Clear glass bowl with polychrome parallel and diagonal canes, the bowl somewhat flattened and the ends pulled out and down, resembling a toreador hat, and mounted on a clear scalloped foot. L 10 in. (25.4 cm.) unsigned

Opposite page:
1.41 **Venini "Morandiane" decanter with stopper** Waisted bottle with stopper in vertical stripes of red and teal green. H. 18 in. (45.7 cm.) acid stamp VENINI MURANO ITALIA and with paper label. *Photo Courtesy of Christie's*

1.43 **Venini fazzoletto bowls** Four small bowls in the popular handkerchief form, each of clear glass with two colors of opaque canes (rods) —yellow and turquoise, black and turquoise, pink and turquoise, and yellow and black. average H. 2¾ in. (7 cm.) acid stamp VENINI MURANO (no room on narrow rim for ITALIA)

1.44 **Detail of black and yellow fazzoletto**

1.45 **Mezza filigrana pinched vase and bowl** Turquoise and copper metallic (aventurine) parallel diagonal stripes on pinched and folded bowl and vase, typical of fifties asymmetrical shapes. vase H. 2¼ in. (5.7 cm.) bowl D. 3½ in. (9 cm.) unsigned

1.46 **Detail of parallel rods**

1.47 **Blue and green striped bowl** Heavy clear glass bowl with blue and green canes radiating from the center, probably Muranese. D. 7⅛ in. (18.1 cm.) unsigned

1.48 **Red and white rimmed plate** Flat plate with rimmed edge in clear glass with canes of red and lattimo radiating from the center. D. 5¼ in. (13.3 cm.) unsigned *Collection of Robert Josephson*

1.49 **Blue and orange ruffled bowl** Clear glass with wide stripes in orange, blue, and lattimo spiraling from the center and becoming narrow toward the ruffled rim. D. 10 in. (25.4 cm.) unsigned *Collection of Robert Josephson*

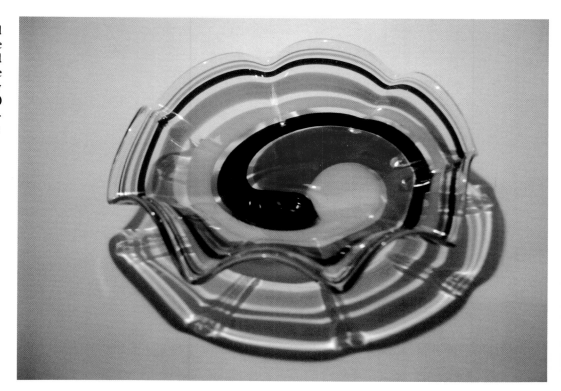

1.50 **Yellow and gold spiral bowl** Clear glass bowl with stripes spiraling from the center in lattimo, aventurine, and yellow. D. 7⅛ in. (18.1 cm.) unsigned

1.51 **Three small mezza filigrana vases** Two small vases of clear glass with turquoise and white mezza filigrana, and one in clear glass with pink and white diagonal stripes and molded foot, each with a thin aventurine applied rim, and resembling 19th century examples made in both Murano and Clichy, France (or possibly of that period). turquoise H. 2 in. (5.1 cm.) pink H. 2⅜ in. (6 cm.) unsigned

1.53 **Multicolored mezza filigrana vase** Clear glass vase with multi-colored rods in a parallel diagonal striped pattern with clear foot and trailed scallops up the two sides. H. 4½ in. (11.4 cm.) unsigned

1.52 **Mezza filigrana vase** Small footed vase of clear glass with parallel diagonal stripes in a pattern of three lattimo and one amber. H. 3¼ in. (8.3 cm) unsigned

1.54 **Pink striped vase** Vase in flattened ovoid form with narrow neck, the clear glass with canes in pink and aventurine, with clear applied foot and ruffled collar. H. 5¾ in. (14.6 cm.) unsigned

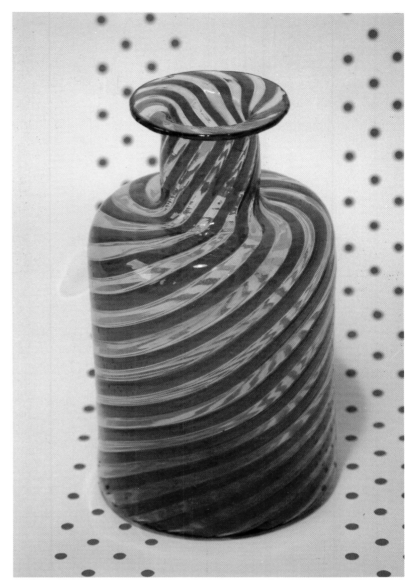

1.55 **Spiderweb bowls** Thick sculptural clear glass bowls each with a scalloped cane spiraling from the center and resembling a spider web, the smaller bowl in pink and the larger in lattimo. D. 5 in. (12.7 cm.) larger D. 6⅜ in. (16.2 cm.) unsigned

1.56 **Red and yellow mezza filigrana bottle** Barrel-shaped bottle with narrow neck and flared lip of yellow and red canes forming diagonal stripes (stopper missing). H. 7 in. (17.8 cm.) unsigned

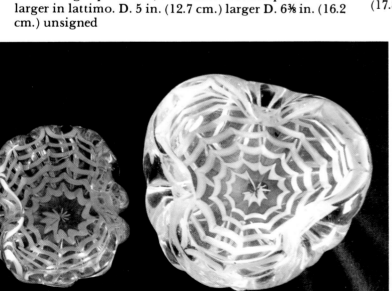

1.57 Venini "Pezzato" vase by Fulvio Bianconi Cylindrical vase in blue, red, and yellow-green patchwork, with inner lattimo layers. H. 11¾in. (29 cm.) acid stamp VENINI MURANO ITALIA *Photo courtesy of Sotheby's*

1.58 left **Barovier & Toso torso-shaped vase by Fulvio Bianconi** Light blue bubbled glass in the form of a female torso, with two handles bent like arms against the body. H. 6¾ in. (17 cm.) unsigned

center **Venini "Pezzato Arlechino" vase by Fulvio Bianconi** Waisted cylindrical form, the asymmetrical patchwork in vivid red, blue, green, and clear glass. H. 9½ in. (24 cm.)

right **Venini "Scozzese" vase by Fulvio Bianconi** Flared cylindrical form, the clear glass internally decorated with tomato red and brown intersecting diagonal stripes and turquoise vertical stripes. H. 7¾ in. (19.5 cm.) acid stamp VENINI MURANO ITALIA *Photo courtesy of Christie's*

1.59 **Barovier & Toso murrina vase** Short vase of waisted cylindrical form with scalloped rim in regular patchwork checkerboard pattern of cobalt blue squares with pink trefoil center outlined in lattimo, alternating with lattimo squares with pink six petaled flower with yellow center and green stem. H. 2⅞ in. (7.3 cm.) D. 3¾in. (9.5 cm.) unsigned.

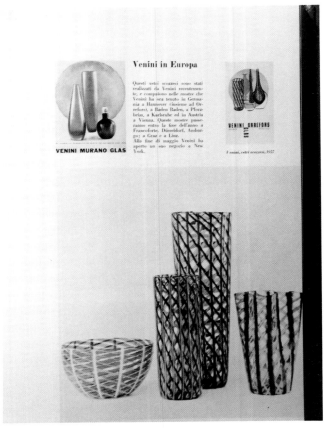

Venini "Vetri Scozzesi," 1957 *Photo courtesy of ©Domus*
(332:43, July 1957)

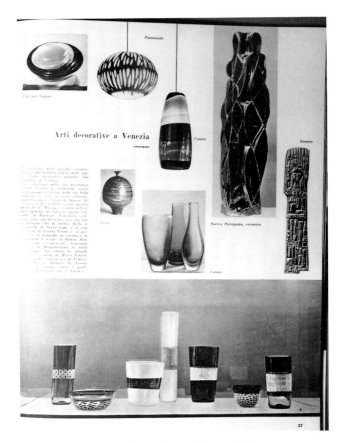

Venini glass and other decorative art *Photo courtesy
of ©Domus (324:37, Nov. 1956)*

Venini bottles and vases *Photo courtesy of
©Domus ((361:41, Dec. 1959)*

Opposite page:

1.60 Barovier & Toso "Millefili" vase by Ercole Barovier
Cylindrical vase in murrhine glass of shades of orange in
the "thousand threads" pattern alternating with pale
orange rectangles, resulting in one of the most refined and
typical examples of tastes of the 1950s. H. 10 in. (25.5 cm.)
engraved signature ERCOLE BAROVIER 1956 *Photo
courtesy of Sotheby's*

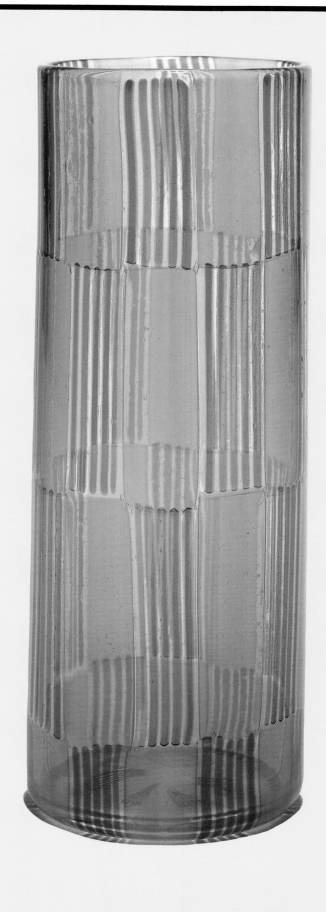

1.61 left **Barovier & Toso "Parabolica" vase designed by Ercole Barovier** Cylindrical murrhine glass vase of opalescent turquoise and grey basketweave patchwork outlined in violet. H. 7¼ in. (18.5 cm.) engraved TO ZINO, MY VERY GOOD FRIEND, ERCOLE

center **Barovier & Toso "Tessere Ambra" vase designed by Ercole Barovier** Cylindrical vase of murrhine glass of amber sections outlined in violet in a basketweave patchwork pattern. H. 10 in. (25.5 cm.)

right **Barovier & Toso "Parabolica" vase by Ercole Barovier** Short cylindrical vase of murrhine glass in opalescent sea-green and grey patches in a basketweave pattern. H. 5⅛ in. (13 c.) engraved **ERCOLE BAROVIER** 1960 *Photo courtesy of Sotheby's*

1.62 **Barovier & Toso "Murrino" bowl, vase, and basket designed by Ercole Barovier** Round bowl with flared top and applied foot, bulbous vase with narrow cylindrical neck, and tapered rectangular basket, the vetro murrino design of irregular rectangular slices of cane in clear glass with gold surrounded by lattimo, amethyst, and aquamarine, and designed in 1948. bowl H. 3⅛ in. (9 cm.) vase H. 7 in. (17.5 cm.) basket H. 3⅛ in. (8 cm.) *Collection of Angelo Barovier and photo courtesy of AB/Barovier & Toso*

1.64 Barovier & Toso "Diamantati" vases and bowl designed by Ercole Barovier Melon shaped vase with narrow cylindrical neck, globular vase narrowing to short flared neck, and asymmetrical bowl flaring at the top, each with multicolor transparent rectangular murrhine arranged in vertical columns with a single color for each column, creating the effect of stained glass windows; the series was designed by Ercole Barovier in 1968 and exhibited at the Venice Biennale in that year. left H. 11⅜ in. (28 cm.) center H. 6¾ in.(17 cm.) right H. 7⅞ in. (20 cm.) *Collection of Angelo Barovier and photo courtesy of AB/Barovier & Toso*

Opposite page:

1.63 Barovier & Toso "Saturneo" bottle and vase designed by Ercole Barovier The bottle with circular base tapering to a long narrow neck, and the vase with flared shoulders tapering to a circular base and with narrow cylindrical neck, decorated in spiral amethyst murrhine arranged in vertical rows alternating with triple lattimo stripes. bottle H. 9½ in. (24 cm.) vase H. 11¾ in. (30 cm.) *Collection of Angelo Barovier and photo courtesy of AB/Barovier & Toso.*

1.65 Barovier & Toso "Oriente" bottle, bowl, and vase designed by Ercole Barovier Gourd shaped bottle with narrow cylindrical neck, round bowl with applied latticino rim, and bulbous vase with narrow cylindrical neck, in polychrome stained glass window effect in vibrant reds, oranges, and blues, designed by Ercole Barovier in 1940 and shown at the Venice Biennale and Milan Triennale. bottle H. 11⅜ in. (29 cm.) bowl D. 5⅛ in. (13 cm.) vase H. 4⅜ in. (11 cm.) *Collection of Angelo Barovier and photo courtesy AB/Barovier & Toso.*

1.66 **Aureliano Toso "Oriente" vase designed by Dino Martens** Tapered and flattened cylindrical vase with flared and folded top, internally decorated with filigree, murrhine, aventurine, and patches of red, white, blue, and yellow, encased in clear glass, resulting in an abstract pattern that seems to embody all that is fifties in fifties glass. H. 9 in. (23 cm.) unsigned

1.67 **Detail of "Oriente" vase**

1.68 **Detail of A.V.E.M. vase**

1.69 **A.V.E.M. vase possibly designed by Anzolo Fuga**
Cylindrical vase flattened and flaring at the rim, of thick
sea-green glass internally decorated with bits of colored
canes, filigree, silver foil, and gold foil, then encased in
clear glass. H. 12½ in. (31.7 cm.) unsigned

1.72 **Small murrina vase** Three-sided vase of thick clear glass internally decorated with silver foil, latticino, and murrhine. H. 2¼ in. (5.7 cm.) unsigned, but probably by A.V.E.M.

1.70 **Pear and apple paperweight** Clear glass paperweight in the form of a pear and an apple with applied stem and leaf, internally decorated with polychrome canes, bits of glass ribbon, and latticino. Pear. H. 4⅞ in. (12.4 cm.) unsigned, but probably by A.V.E.M.

1.71 **A.V.E.M. pear detail**

1.73 **Cylindrical vase, possibly by A.V.E.M.** Small vase of clear glass internally decorated with silver foil, latticino, and murrhine. H. 3 in. (7.6 cm.) unsigned

1.74 **Sculptural bowl, probably by A.V.E.M.** Thick sea-green glass internally decorated with silver foil, latticino, and murrhine, encased in clear glass. Possibly designed by Dino Martens. D. 7¾ in. (19.7 cm.) unsigned

1.75 **Detail of bowl**

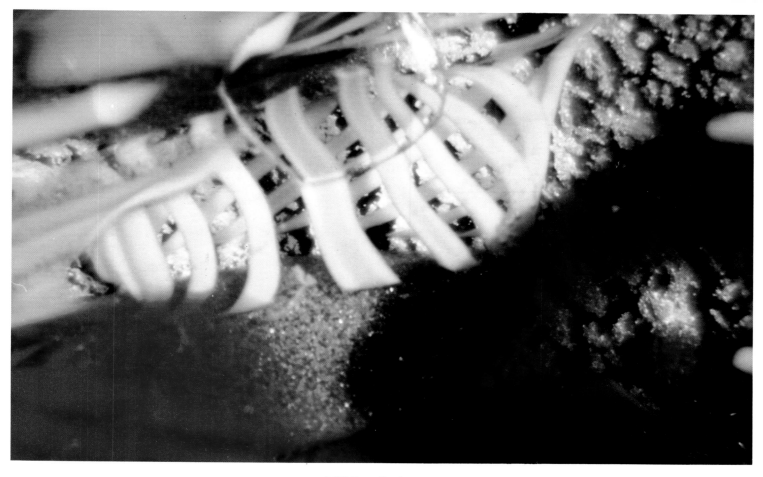

1.76 **Detail of bowl**

1.77 **Multicolored bowl** Black glass bowl with four lobes in a typically fifties biomorphic shape with colorful inclusions of glass bits and silver foil. L. 10½ in. (27.7 cm.) unsigned *Collection of Shirley Friedland*

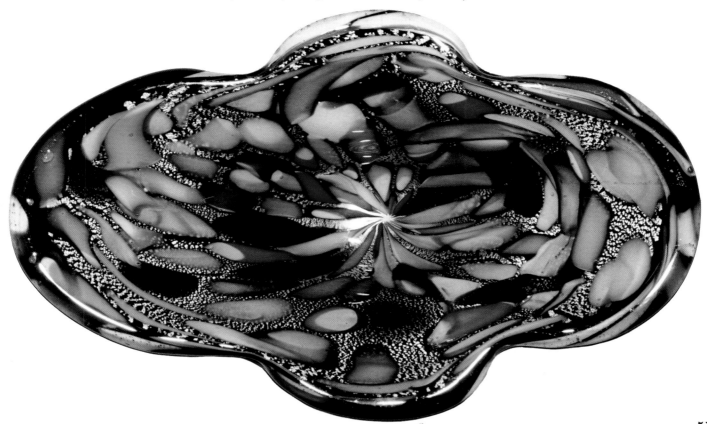

1.78 Sculptural bowl with colored inclusions Thick clear glass bowl or plate in elongated flattened shape internally decorated with bits of colored glass canes, and gold and silver foil. L 10 in. (25.4 cm.) unsigned *Collection of Shirley Friedland*

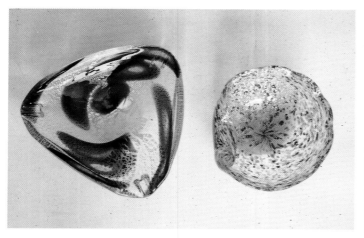

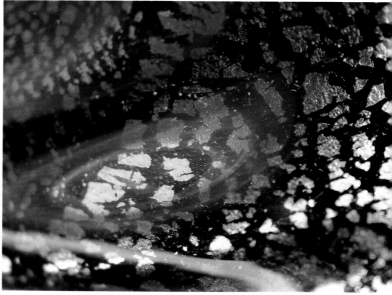

1.79 Triangular bowl and folded bowl with silver Clear glass bowl with red, purple, yellow, and silver leaf inclusions in a triangular shape, together with scalloped bowl with side folded inward, of clear glass internally decorated with polychrome and silver leaf bits. D. 7¾ in. (19.7 cm.) scalloped D 6¼ in. (16 cm.)

1.80 Detail of triangular bowl

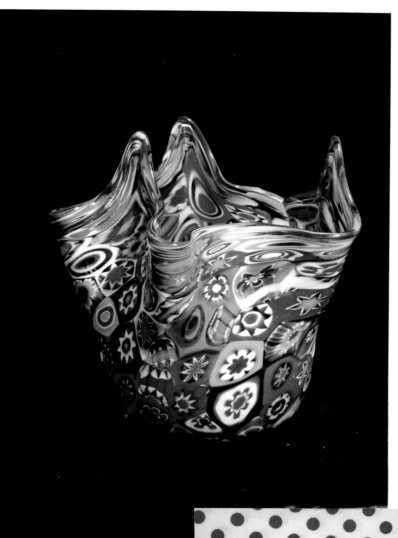

1.81 **Millefiori fazzoletto vase** Handkerchief-shaped vase of clear glass (without the acid-dipped matte finish given to many recently-made small millefiori items) with slices of multicolored canes fused together in the "thousand flower" or millefiori pattern before the vessel is blown into its final shape. H. 4½ in. (11.4 cm.) paper label LA SERNISSIMA MURANO ITALY

1.82 **Folded bowl with spots of color** Cased layers of white, turquoise, and clear glass, the white layer internally decorated with spotty patches of polychrome and metallic pieces, folded inward on two sides. D. 7 in. (17.8 cm.) unsigned

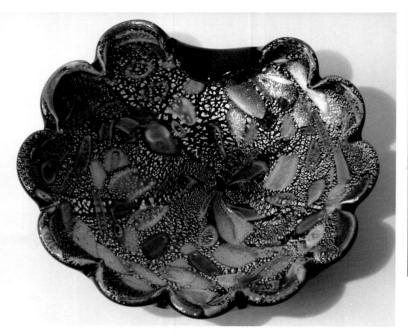

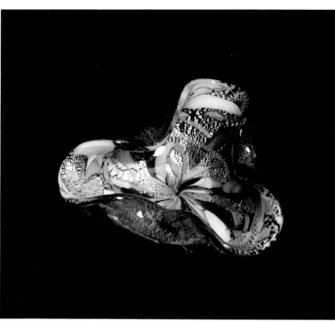

1.85 Three-sided folded bowl Amoeboid shaped bowl of turquoise glass internally decorated with silver foil and colored murrhine, encased in clear glass, folded in on three sides. D. 6¼ in. (15.9 cm.) unsigned

1.83 Scalloped bowl Black glass internally decorated with silver leaf, copper metallic powder, and multicolored murrhine, encased in clear glass, with one of 12 rim scallops folded inward. D. 9½ in. (24.1 cm.) unsigned *Collection of Shirley Friedland*

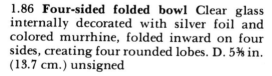

1.86 Four-sided folded bowl Clear glass internally decorated with silver foil and colored murrhine, folded inward on four sides, creating four rounded lobes. D. 5⅜ in. (13.7 cm.) unsigned

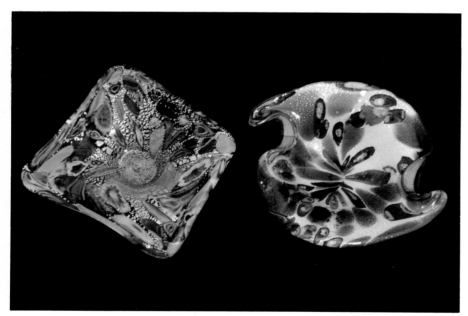

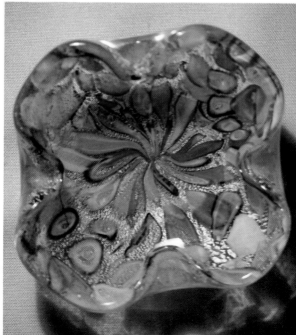

1.84 Two biomorphic blob bowls The left in clear glass in an asymmetrical stretched square shape with silver foil and murrhine inclusions; the right of white glass internally decorated with silver foil and colored murrhine, in an amoeboid shape with pulled and folded ends. D. 8⅝ in. (21.9 cm.) D. 8¼ in. (21 cm.) unsigned

1.89 Yellow boomerang plate Thick yellow glass internally decorated with slices of colored murrhine, a version of the popular fifties boomerang. L. 9⅞ in. (25.1 cm.) unsigned.

1.87 Boomerang plate Clear glass internally decorated with pale turquoise swirls, in a biomorphic boomerang shape; versions of this three-lobed stretched form were popularized in the fifties and frequently used in a variety of applied and graphic arts. L. 10 in. (25.4 cm.) unsigned. *Collection of Shirley Friedland*

1.90 Dresser set by Archimede Seguso Covered jar and atomizer, each with exaggerated melon-like vertical reeding, of pearly white glass patterned with turquoise diamond shapes and metallic flecks. jar D. atomizer H. 5⅛ in. (13 cm.) jar D. 4 in. (10.2 cm.) paper labels ARCHIMEDE SEGUSO MURANO MADE IN ITALY and MADE IN MURANO ITALY. The use of two separate labels suggests that pieces with only the scalloped MADE IN MURANO ITALY label are also by Seguso.

1.88 Finger bowl Clear glass with multicolored glass inclusions and pairs of red glass finger-like projections around the rim. D. 8¾ in. (22.2 cm.) unsigned. *Collection of Lois and George Epstein*

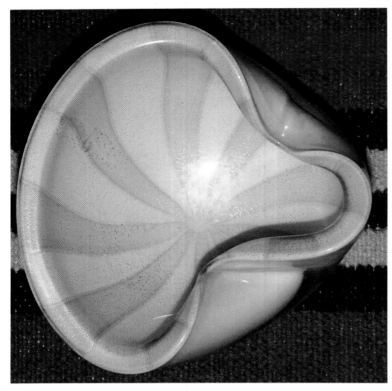

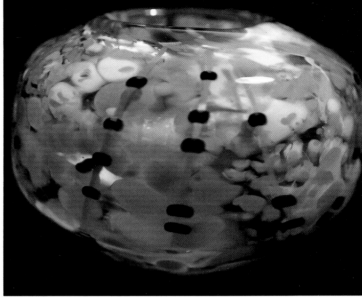

1.91 Barbini folded pink and white bowl Alternating pink and white stripes radiating from the center and encased in a thick layer of clear glass, with two sides folded inward by the firm of Alfredo Barbini. D. 6⅜ in. (16.2 cm.) unsigned

1.93 Ovoid vase with purple spots Flattened globular vase of thick clear glass internally decorated with spots of pastel colors and pink strings with purple beads, possibly by Barovier and Toso. D. 4¼ in. (11.4 cm.) unsigned

1.94 Molded stacking ashtrays Since Murano glass is known for being hand-formed, (in most cases free blown), it is surprising to find molded pieces. These marbelized ashtrays of green, yellow, and metallic glass embedded in opaque black glass are molded in graduated sizes that stack into each other. L. 4 in. (10.2 cm.), 5½ in. (14 cm.), 7 in. (17.8 cm.) molded mark ITALY

1.92 Four Barbini biomorphic bowls Two with pale turquoise and white striped and two pale pink and white striped biomorphic bowls. average D. 6⅜ in. (16.2 cm.)

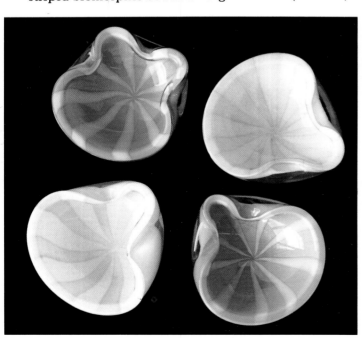

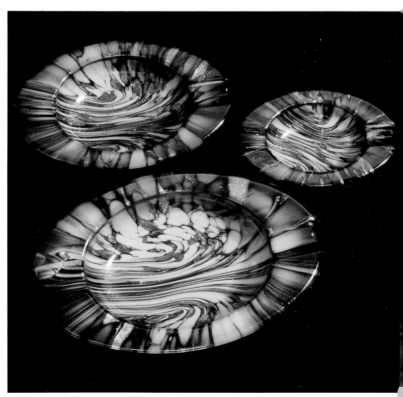

1.95 **Tortoise shell bowl and vase** Clear glass internally decorated with brown to resemble tortoise shell, the vase of a globular shape, and the bowl a half globe. H. vase 3⅛ in. (8 cm.) D. bowl 6½ in. (16.5 cm.) unsigned

1.96 **Tortoise shell figures** Four hollow abstract figures of clear glass internally decorated in shades of brown to imitate tortoise shell. tallest H. 5 in. (12.7 cm) paper label HAND MADE GENUINE VENETIAN GLASS VETRO ARTISTICO VENEZIANA MADE IN MURANO ITALY

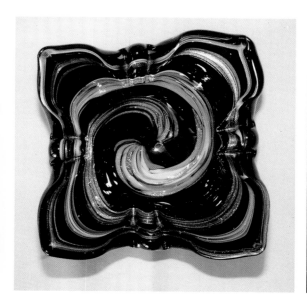

1.97 **Four-lobed bowl** Black glass with polychrome swirls and copper metallic inclusions. D. 9 in. (11.7 cm.) paper label MADE IN ITALY

1.98 **Turquoise and gold bowls** One bowl of triangular shape with end folded inward, of clear bullicante (bubbled) glass with turquoise and gold metallic scalloped swirls; the other of round form in clear glass internally decorated with a gold metallic sunburst radiating from the center with turquoise spots, possibly by Barovier & Toso. D 5½ in. (14 cm.) circular D. 4¾ in. (12.1 cm.) unsigned

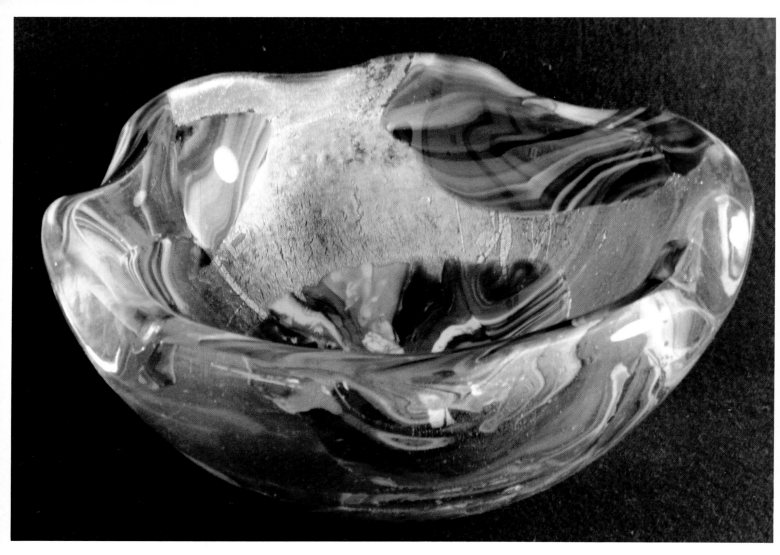

1.99 Calcedonio bowl, possibly by Archimede Seguso Heavy thick clear glass bowl internally decorated with patches of color simulating chalcedony, a type of agate, and metallic particles. D. 7 in. (17.8 cm.) unsigned.

1.100 Calcedonio detail

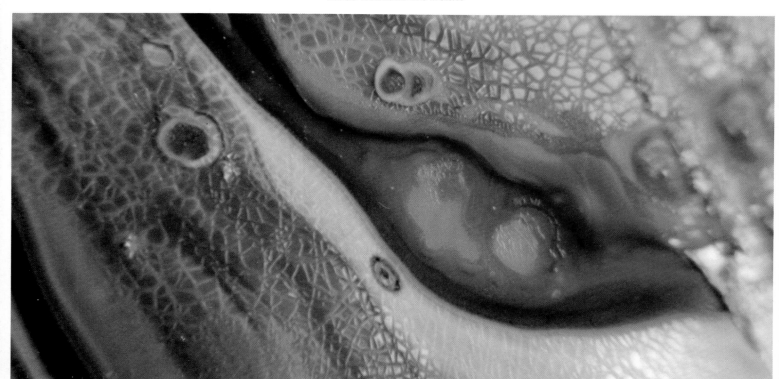

1.101 **Barovier & Toso "Neolitica" vases designed by Ercole Barovier** Vase with wide base tapering to a long cylindrical neck, a bulbous vase with a short narrow neck, and a cylindrical vase with straight sides curving slightly to a narrow base, each of opaque amethyst, white, and earth tone scalloped rows resembling a natural hardstone, of the "Neolitica" series designed by Ercole Barovier in 1954. H. 15⅜ in. (39 cm.), 7⅞ in. (20 cm.), 9¼ in. (23.5 cm) *Collection of Angelo Barovier and photo courtesy of AB/Barovier & Toso*

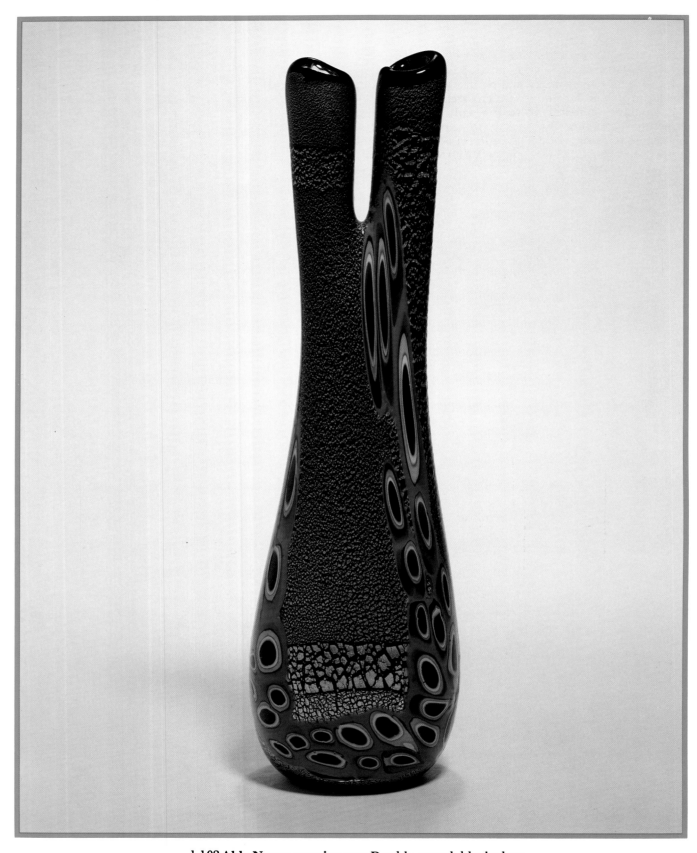

1.102 Aldo Nason murrina vase Double-mouth black glass vase internally decorated with yellow, white, and blue murrhine in a turquoise ground, with adjacent areas of gold leaf, designed by Aldo Nason and made at the Aldo Nason Glassworks. H. 15⅜ in. (39 cm.) *Photo courtesy of Sotheby's*

1.103 Venini "Vetro a Murrine" vase by Carlo and Tobia Scarpa Narrowing form with squared base and straight sides with rounded corners, ending in a scalloped rim in black-purple and lattimo glass. The technique, used by the Romans, consists of fusing colored canes and sometimes grinding the surface to expose the cores, reheating, recasing, and blowing the vessel into its final shape. H. 12¾ in. (32 cm.) paper VENINI label *Photo courtesy of Christie's*

Venini bowl in vetro murrina, 1955 *Photo courtesy of ©Domus (361:38/39 insert, Dec. 1959)*

1.104 Archimede Seguso "Vetro a Piume" vase Flattened pear shape vase, the clear yellow glass internally decorated in white filigree feather motif, an example of one of the most famous Seguso series of the 1950s. H. 14¾ in. (27.5 cm.) *Photo Courtesy of Christie's*

1.105 left **Three tall Vistosi bottle vases by Peter Pelzel** Each vase of slender cylindrical form narrowing to a short neck, two in sapphire blue and one in pale grey, each with a double band of irregular rectangular shapes, in two shades of dark blue on the blue vases and in green and black on the gray vase. H. 17⅛ in. (43.5 cm.), H. 13⅜ in. (34 cm.), H. 16⅛ in. (41 cm.) paper VISTOSI label on two

center left **Venini "Spicchi" bottle designed by Fulvio Bianconi and Massimo Vignelli** Elongated gourd shape with an asymmetrical rim and irregular vertical stripes in pink, purple, and turquoise. H. 14½ in. (37 cm.) acid stamped VENINI MURANO ITALIA

center right **Venini "Murrine" vase designed by Fulvio Bianconi** Flattened ovoid shape with asymmetrical tapering cylindrical leaning neck with glass pulled to a protruding knotty point at the shoulder on one side, in clear glass internally decorated in a random pattern of cobalt blue, ruby red, and turquoise murrina splashes. H. 12⅝ in. (32 cm.) acid stamp VENINI MURANO ITALIA

right **Archimede Seguso "Compisizione Piume" carafe** U-shaped body ending in a curled handle on one side and a pointed curving spout on the other, the clear glass internally decorated with coral feather motifs. H. 11⅜ in. (29 cm.) unsigned, but others of the series have a paper label *Photo courtesy of Christie's*

1.106 left **A.V.E.M. vase designed by Luciano Ferro**
Irregular oval-shaped vase with asymmetrical bulbous
oval neck in pale blue glass internally decorated with
trapped copper wire bows and splashed with green
yellow, and purple. H. 8⅝ in. (22 cm.)

center **Venini vase by Ludovico de Santillano** Tear-
shaped vase with narrow opening at the neck in gray glass
with irregular applied white dripping stripes running
from the neck to the middle. H. 8⅛ in. (20.5 cm.) acid
stamp VENINI MURANO ITALIA

right **Large A.V.E.M. bottle by Luciano Ferro** Ovoid
shape narrowing to a small cylindrical neck and
asymmetrical rim, divided into two color areas of pale
blue upper half and ruby red lower half, with a profusion
of tiny internal air bubbles throughout, and an irregular
band of murrina target motifs in pale amber and dark blue
around the middle. H. 15⅜ in. (39 cm.) *Photo courtesy of
Christie's*

Opposite page:

1.107 **Large A.V.E.M. vase by Luciano Ferro** Rose to
pumpkin color with celery green on one side and decorated
with red, yellow, and blue murrhine on the other, with
clear base of cut cone shape with inclusion of red teardrop.
H. 19¼ in. (49 cm.) engraved on the base COLLEZIONE
LUCIANO FERRO 1953 *Photo courtesy of Sotheby's*

1.108 **A.V.E.M.** **vase** Spheroidal shape with long neck widened at the mouth, of clear cristallo with gold leaf decorated with an irregular blue band and polychrome murrhine. H. 10¼ in. (26 cm.) *Photo courtesy of Sotheby's*

1.109 **Pear-shaped vase possibly by Ercole Barovier** Clear glass filled with copper metallic particles, the pear-shaped vase with vertical fluting on the exterior and diagonal ridges on the interior, together creating a diamond effect, and resembling "Cordonato Oro" by Ercole Barovier. H. 9⅛ in. (23.2 cm.) unsigned

1.110 **Archimede Seguso three-sided vase** Heavy clear glass vase with three flat sides, one internally decorated with gold flecks, the other two in sfumato mist of plum shading from light to dark with gold sprinkles, designed by Archimede Seguso. H. 9¾ in. (24.8 cm.) unsigned

Opposite page:

1.111 **Sommerso vases** Two flattened asymmetrical teardrop-shaped vases with red center encased in thick amber glass with a liquid appearance, probably designed by Flavio Poli for Seguso Vetri d' Arte. H. 8⅛ in. (20.6 cm.) unsigned

1.113 **Sommerso vase** Flattened symmetrical teardrop shape with cobalt blue interior encased in thick pale blue glass, possibly by Flavio Poli for Seguso Vetri d'Arte. H. 11¼ in. (28.6 cm.) unsigned

1.114 **Somerso vase** Round water droplet form with red-orange shape encased in thick clear glass. H. 6 in. (15.2 cm.) unsigned

Opposite page:

1.112 **Sommerso teardrop vase** Flattened symmetrical red water droplet shape incased in thick pale yellow-green glass, probably designed by Flavio Poli for Seguso Vetri d'Arte. H. 9¼ in. (23.5 cm.) unsigned

1.115 **Target teardrop vase** Round teardrop-shaped vase with flared rim in clear glass internally decorated on one side with a droplet-shaped target of pink, blue, orange, and green bands, similar to an example by Ermanno Toso (Heiremans, cat. no. 160). H. 7¾ in. (19.7 cm.) unsigned

1.117 **Geode bowl** Thick clear glass encasing cobalt blue in a very even and round form resembling a geode sliced in two. D. 6¼ in. (15.9 cm.) unsigned

1.116 **Sommerso dresser set** Heavy sculptural dresser set of a round covered jar with a false stopper attached to the lid, and two flattened bottles with stoppers, each in thick clear glass encasing turquoise droplet shapes with gold metallic inclusions, with an effect of flowing molten glass, possibly designed by Flavio Poli for Seguso Vetri d'Arte. bottle H. 8¾ in. (22.2 cm.) jar H. 5⅝ in. (14.3 cm.) unsigned

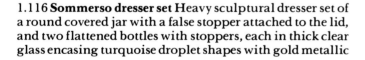

1.118 Alfredo Barbini sommerso vase Heavy sculptural vase of asymmetrical oval body on solid flattened cylindrical elongated foot, with small red bubble encased in four layers of gray and clear glass, textured with fine lines on the surface. H. 10¼ in. (26 cm.) engraved BARBINI and with partial paper label *Photo courtesy of Christie's*

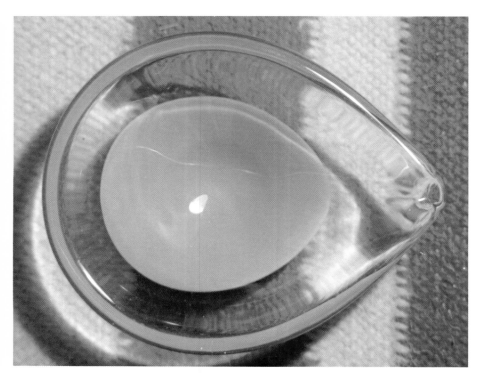

1.119 **Small Venini sommerso bowl** Roundish turquoise form encased in clear glass, forming a teardrop-shaped flattened bowl. D. 4¾ in. (12.1 cm.) acid stamp VENINI MURANO

1.120 **Sommerso flower bowl** Thick clear glass encasing a 12-petaled red-orange flower radiating from the center of a symmetrical round bowl. D. 7½ in. (19 cm.) unsigned

1.121 **Sommerso leaf bowl** Flattened leaf shaped bowl of opaque white and green leaf encased in pale yellow-green leaf shape with stem, and an example of one of the popular sommerso forms being reproduced today and sold as fifties glass. L. 8¾ in. (22.2 cm.) unsigned

1.122 **Cased bowl** Round bowl with pinched end cased in three layers: amber, white, and turquoise. D. 7¾ in. (19.7 cm.) unsigned

1.123 **Folded bowl** Round flattened bowl with one side folded inward, the deep red interior with inclusions of gold flecks, encased in a layer of yellow and another of white glass. D. 7½ in. (19 cm.) unsigned

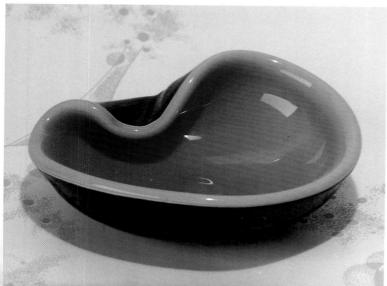

1.124 **Pink and black biomorphic blob** Round bowl folded inward in asymmetrical organic shape, the pink glass cased in black. D. 5⅝ in. (16.8 cm.) unsigned

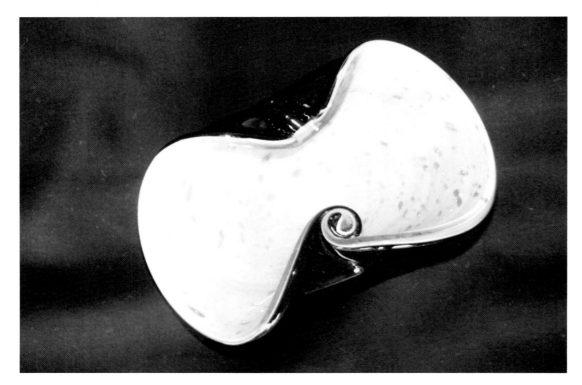

1.125 **Rolled and folded bowl** Turquoise glass with patches of gold leaf, cased in black and clear glass, in a folded and rolled biomorphic shape typical of the many imaginative ashtrays and bowls produced by Barbini and other Murano companies. L. 6½ in. (16.5 cm.) unsigned

1.126 **Three whipped bubble bowls** Heavy sculptural bowls with black glass and gold leaf particles on the interior, encased in thick clear glass filled with minute air bubbles producing a frothy and opaque effect. average D. 5⅜ in. (13.6 cm.) unsigned

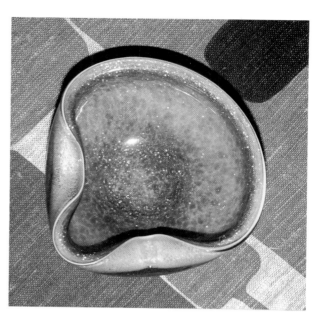

1.127 **Folded bowl** Shades of pink glass encased in clear layer containing air bubbles, and one side folded inward. D. 5 in. (12.7 cm.) unsigned

1.129 **Folded bowl** Clear glass with copper flecks, cased with white and then clear glass, and folded inward on two sides. D. 6¼ in. (15.1 cm.) unsigned

1.128 **Four layer bowl** Kidney shaped bowl cased in four layers: amber, white, black, and clear glass. D. 6 in. (15.2 cm.) unsigned

1.130 **Folded white bowl** Translucent white glass bowl with two opposite sides folded inward. D. 6 in. (15.2 cm.) unsigned

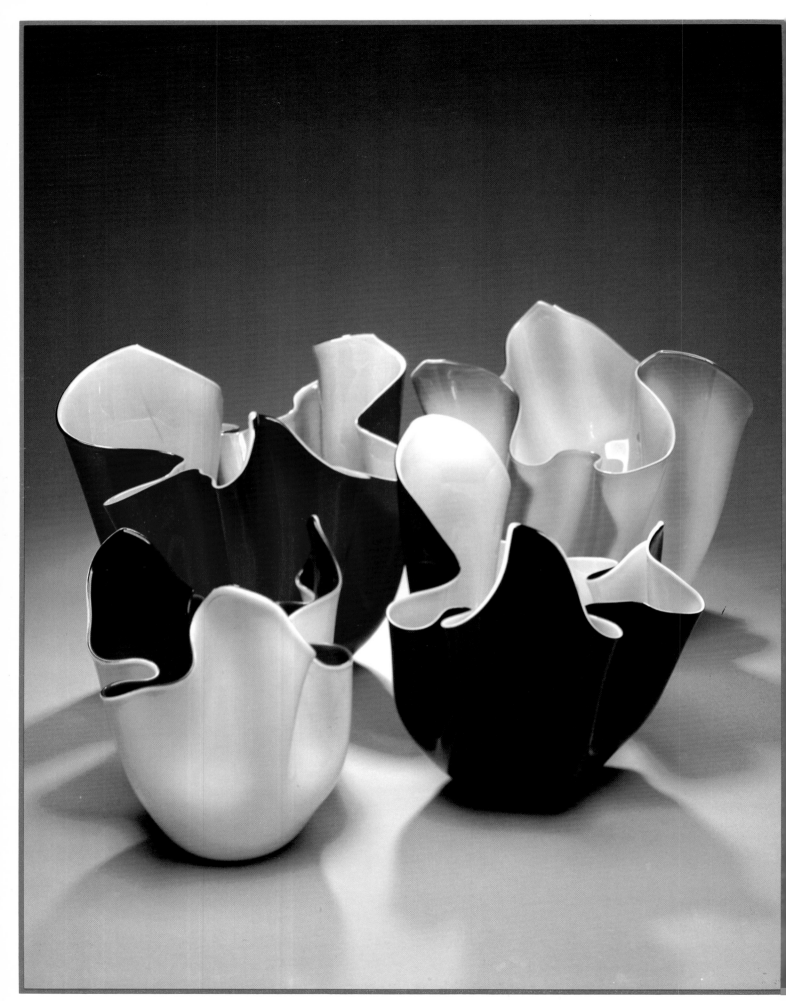

1.132 **Long necked vases** Bulbous vase with long narrow neck of four extremely thin cased layers: pink, white, red, and clear, with round clear glass foot. H. 10¾ in. (27.3 cm.) unsigned

1.133 **Barbini vase** Turquoise-blue glass with metallic flecks, encased in clear glass, the broad shouldered vase waisted above the circular foot. H. 4½ in. (11.4 cm.) paper label VENETIAN MADE BY ALFREDO BARBINI FOR WEIL CERAMICS MURANO ITALY

Opposite page:

1.131 top left **Venini fazzoletto vase designed by Fulvio Bianconi** Irregularly folded handkerchief vase with pale pink interior cased with garnet red. H. 10¼ in. (26 cm.) acid stamp VENINI MURANO ITALIA and with partial paper label

bottom left **Venini fazzoletto vase designed by Fulvio Bianconi** Irregularly folded handkerchief vase in opaque purple cased with white. H. 8¼ in. (21 cm.) acid stamp VENINI MURANO ITALIA

top right **Venini fazzoletto vase designed by Fulvio Bianconi** Irregularly folded handkerchief vase in lattimo glass cased with transparent oyster green. H. 10¼ in. (26 cm.) acid stamp VENINI MURANO ITALIA

bottom right **Venini fazzoletto vase by Fulvio Bianconi** Irregularly folded handkerchief vase of slightly opalescent white glass cased with metallic black. H. 9⅞ in. (25 cm.) acid stamp VENINI MURANO ITALIA *Photo courtesy of Christie's*

1.134 **Two Barbini vases** Each in clear glass filled with copper particles cased over a lattimo interior, the shorter with broad shoulder and waisted above the circular foot, the taller of hourglass shape with applied lattimo trail around the waist; some examples were used to hold cigarette lighters. left H. 4½ in. (11.4 cm.) right H. 6¼ in. (15.9 cm.) unsigned

1.135 **Venini incalmo bottle** Bottle of deep turquoise glass fused to red band in incalmo technique, with yellow stopper (probably a replacement, and the neck has been lowered). H. 10½ in. (26.7 cm.) acid stamp VENINI MURANO ITALIA

1.136 **Starfish centerpiece** Transparent turquoise-blue glass with swirls of gold flecks in the form of a starfish. max H. 22¼ in. (56.5 cm.) unsigned *Courtesy of Michael Joseph Antiques, Cleveland*

1.137 left **Vase attributed to Ferro Lazzarini and design to Flavio Poli** Flattened bulbous emerald-green base with long tapering cylindrical neck and collar in ruby red, with acid treated surface above the base. H. 12⅝ in. (32 cm.) unsigned

center **Salviati vase designed by Luciano Gaspari** Cylindrical bubble shaped vase in pale green, decorated at the neck with a broad trailed irregular band shading from emerald green to blue and turquoise. H. 10 in. (25.5) cm. engraved L. GASPARI SALVIATI

right **Venini vase designed by Thomas Stearns** Asymmetrical bubble shape of pale gray glass shading to blue and darker blue near the rim with a continuous irregular narrow blue band trailed around the top half. H. 9⅞ in. (25 cm.) acid stamp VENINI MURANO ITALIA
Photo courtesy of Christie's

1.138 **Murano vase** Red glass cased with opaque white glass speckled with metallic particles, with black spirals trailing horizontally and red trailed zigzags, mounted on a conical foot internally decorated with metallic particles and red and black threads, with applied gold leafed leaf-shaped handles. H. 7⅝ in. (19.5 cm.) unsigned, but in the manner of Fulvio Bianconi *Photo courtesy of Sotheby's*

1.139 **Aureliano Toso vase designed by Dino Martens**
Black glass vase with compressed body, round depression in the center, asymmetrical elongated spout, and applied swirls on one side. H. 10¼ in. (26 cm.) unsigned *Photo courtesy of Sotheby's*

1.140 front row **Three Venini "vetro groviglio" vases of the "Giada" series designed by Toni Zuccheri** Stoppered decanters, the left two in vivid red-orange (the most typical color) and the right in cobalt blue, internally decorated with copper threads and occasional trapped air bubbles, encased in clear glass; Toni Zuccheri designed this series in 1964 as part of a long collaboration with Venini. left H. 7 in. (18 cm.) paper label VENINI MURANO VENEZIA No. 8663 MADE IN ITALY, center H. 6¼ in. (16 cm.), right H. 5⅞ in. (15 cm.) acid stamp VENINI MURANO ITALIA and paper label VENINI MURANO VENEZIA No. 8665? MADE IN ITALY

center row **Venini "Giada" vase by Toni Zuccheri** Baluster shaped vase with short cylindrical neck of ochre glass internally decorated with copper threads. H. 7⅞ in. (20 cm.) acid stamp VENINI MURANO ITALIA

top row **Three Venini "Giada" bottles** Stoppered bottle-vases, the left of cobalt blue, center of Chinese redorange, and the right of olive green, each internally decorated with copper wire and cased in clear glass. left H. 11¾ in. (30 cm.) acid stamp VENINI MURANO ITALIA and paper label VENINI MURANO VENEZIA MADE IN ITALY, center H. 12¼ in. (31 cm.) paper label VENINI MURANO VENEZIA No. 8666 MADE IN ITALY, right H. 11¾ in. (30cm.) acid stamp VENINI MURANO ITALIA and paper label VENINI MURANO VENEZIA MADE IN ITALY
Photo courtesy of Christie's

1.141 Venini "vetro groviglio" vase of the "Giada" series designed by Toni Zuccheri Bulbous vase with cylindrical neck in red-orange glass internally decorated with copper wire with occasional trapped air bubbles, and cased with clear glass. H. 7½ in. (19 cm.) paper label VENINI S. A. MURANO

1.142 **"Giada" detail**

1.143 **"Giada" detail**

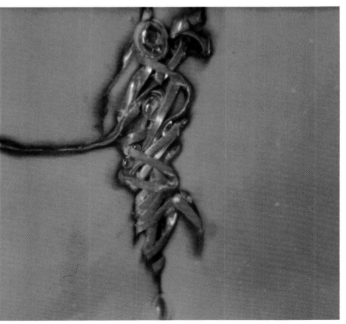

1.144 **Barovier & Toso "Eugenia" lamp bases designed by Ercole Barovier** Bubbled green glass with iridescent surface, the tapered form with one handle on each side, exhibited at the 1952 Venice Biennale. H. 11½ in. (25 cm.) *Photo courtesy of Christie's*

1.145 left **Barovier & Toso "Vaso con Anelli" designed by Ercole Barovier** Flared and flattened cylindrical vase with three applied flat round handles on each side, the clear glass with large regularly placed air bubbles, designed in 1938 by Ercole Barovier. H. 11¾ in. (30 cm.) etched ITALIA

center **Barovier & Toso vase designed by Ercole Barovier** Baluster shape with cylindrical neck and narrow rim, in clear glass decorated with iron filings and other inclusions; this technique was exhibited at the 1952 Venice Biennale and at the 1953 Paris Exposition. H. 7½ in. (19 cm.)

right **Barovier & Toso applied vase designed by Ercole Barovier** Flared flattened cylindrical form with three applied flat round handles on each side, the clear glass with iron filing inclusions. H. 11¾ in. (30 cm.) *Photo courtesy of Christie's*

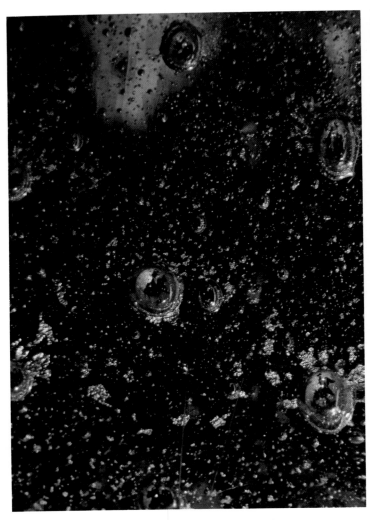

1.146 **Venini bullicante detail**

1.148 **Bullicante vase with trailing** Mottled light and dark gray glass internally decorated with stretched air bubbles, cased with clear glass, the tapered cylindar form with a trailed rope of clear glass. H. 8½ in. (21.6 cm.) unsigned, possibly by Archimede Seguso

1.147 **Venini bullicante bowl** Transparent turquoise glass internally decorated with gold metallic flecks and regularly spaced air bubbles. D. 3 in. (7.6 cm.) acid stamp VENINI MURANO MADE IN ITALY

1.149 **Mottled orange pulegosa vase** Thick transluscent glass with slightly iridescent finish, internally decorated with asymmetrical patches of orange and irregular air bubbles, the wide shouldered bulbous form tapering to a circular base. H. 8⅜ in. (21.3 cm.) paper label MADE IN ITALY

1.150 **Bullicante paperweight pears** Two sommerso paperweights in the form of pears with hollow red glass centers encased in thick heavy pale yellow glass filled with regularly placed air bubbles, one side cut and ground in order to set the pear on its side, with applied deep green stem and leaf. H. 6⅜ in. (16.2 cm.) paper label GENUINE VENETIAN GLASS MADE IN MURANO ITALY

1.151 **Kidney shaped bowl and round vase** Bowl of deep red with gold metallic flecks encased in thick clear glass with tiny air bubbles whipped into the batch and creating a frothy effect, then cased with clear glass; the globular vase with black interior and same bubbly casing. L. 6½ in. (16.5 cm.) round H. 3⅜ in. (8.6 cm.) unsigned but same series as lot no. 31 of Treadway auction attributed to Venini.

1.152 **Yellow bullicante vase** Flared cylindrical vase of clear glass internally decorated with bright yellow in a loose basket weave and regular air bubbles. H. 5 in. (12.7 cm.) unsigned

1.153 **Lattimo leaf dish** Milk glass encased in clear with bullicante and metallic particles, in the form of a leaf with zigzag edge. L. 13 in. (33 cm.) unsigned

1.154 **Barbini bullicante bowl** Triple-layered cased glass in bright orange, lattimo, and clear with regular trapped air bubbles, rolled at the ends and folded inward on two sides in an organic shape typical of the many bowls and ashtrays of the period. L. 9⅝ in. (24,6 cm.) unsigned but pictured in the Barbini company catalog.

1.155 **Cased bullicante bowl** Lattimo glass with bullicante and gold flecks radiating from the center, encased in thick red and a layer of clear glass, folded inward on one side in a biomorphic shape. D. 6⅜ in. (16.2 cm.) unsigned

1.156 **Barovier & Toso "Barbarico" vases designed by Ercole Barovier** The left vase folded over as sculpture with applied animal head and neck, the right an asymmetric vase with solid flat handle and spout, both in a techniques of "colors without fusion" in which the rustic texture of black and gold sits on the surface; Ercole Barovier designed this famous series in 1951 and showed in an international glass exhibition in Paris in that year. left H. 8⅝ in. (22 cm.) right H. 7¼ in. (18.5 cm.) *Collection of Angelo Barovier and photo courtesy of AB/Barovier & Toso*

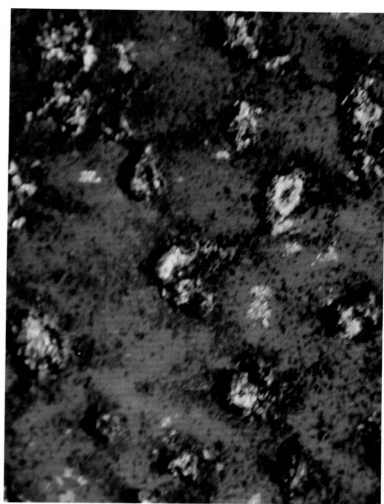

1.157 **Pair of Barovier & Toso "Barbarico" vases designed by Ercole Barovier** Tapered four-sided vases with applied circular foot, with rustic external texture of black and gold leaf, of the famous "Barbarico" series designed by Ercole Barovier in 1951. H. 12¾ in. (32.4 cm.) paper label BAROVIER & TOSO MURANO MADE IN ITALY

1.158 **"Barbarico" detail**

1.159 **Textured vase and filigrana bowl** Small flared cylindrical vase with heavily textured surface (resembling Barbarico) of brown drips on aventurine glass; the filigree bowl with parallel stripes of threadlike aventurine. vase H. 3½ in. (8.9 cm.) bowl D. 5⅛ in. (13 cm.) unsigned, but the vase may be by Salviati circa 1880-1900 (Mentasti 1982 p. 239) and the bowl may be by Venini.

Opposite page:

1.160 left Venini "Vetro Battuto" goblet designed by Tobia Scarpa and Ludovico de Santillana Cylindrical stem and rounded bowl with undulating rim is in pale yellow with a martelé finish. H. 11⅜ in. (29 cm.) inscribed VENINI ITALIA

right Venini "Vetro Battuto" dish designed by Tobia Scarpa and Ludovico de Santillana Flared shallow bowl with undulating rim in pale peach with martelé finish. H. 11 in. (28 cm.) inscribed VENINI MURANO ITALIA
Photo courtesy of Christie's

1.161 Group of 21 Venini "Vetro Inciso" vases designed by Paolo Venini This group represents one of several techniques developed by Venini in which the surface is cut or textured after the glass has cooled. In "Vetro Inciso," a surface of fine parallel grooves is incised by abrasion, and it was introduced in 1956 by Paolo Venini and then exhibited at the XXVIII Venice Biennale. The vessels pictured range in color from dull greens to deep oranges and include bottles and vases both with and without stoppers. Heights range from 4½ in. (12 cm.) for the squat orange ginger jar at front center to 17¼ in. (44 cm.) for the dull green vase at right rear. Signatures include the acid stamp VENINI MURANO ITALIA and/or paper labels VENINI S. A. MURANO or VENINI MURANO VENEZIA MADE IN ITALY. *Photo courtesy of Christie's*

1.162 Group of 18 Venini "Vetro Inciso" bottles and bowls designed by Paolo Venini This technique of incising the surface with fine lines is one of several developed by various designers for Venini, in which the cooled surface of the glass vessel is textured by cutting, abrasion, or other means. These assorted bowls, vases, and stoppered bottles range in color from shades of blue, green, and turquoise to brown. The tallest, center rear, is 20 in. (51 cm.). Signatures include the acid stamp VENINI MURANO ITALIA and paper label VENINI MURANO VENEZIA MADE IN ITALY. *Photo courtesy of Christie's*

Venini Inciso *Photo courtesy of © Domus (361:34, Dec. 1959)*

FIGURAL AND SCULPTURAL

1.163 **Musician figurines** Male guitarist and female tambourine player in clear glass with orange costumes covered in gold leaf, with black glass accents of hat, necklace, and instrument trim, mounted on circular bases, probably by Barovier & Toso in the 1940s. H. 12½ in. (31.7 cm.) unsigned

1.164 **Character figurine** Male figure with black glass face and forearms, dressed in a turquoise costume and top hat, with clear glass ruffles, lattimo sash and trailing from the knees down, on a circular clear base with gold leaf. These figurines were usually made in pairs of male and female characters throughout the 40s and 50s. H. 12 in. (30.5 cm.) unsigned

1.165 **Figure with turban and tray of fruit** Male figure with black glass face, forearms, and shoes, with lattimo turban and torso, vivid red costume, tray of multicolored fruit, clear glass with gold leaf ruffles and circular base. H. 13½ in. (34.3 cm.) unsigned

1.166 Salviati fish sculpture designed by Loredano Rosin Heavy glass sculpture of stylized fish in clear glass with amber tail and face, the eyes cut concave and round, and mounted on an abstract base of three layers —clear and two shades of turquoise glass. H. 13⅝ in. (34.8 cm) paper label remnant MADE IN ITALY SALVIATI E MURANO and engraved signature L. Rosin

1.167 Bullicante fish group The two pink fish are encased in thick clear glass in the sommerso technique, with metallic inclusions and bullicante, mounted on a heavy rock-like base with protrusions. This 40s style is more naturalistic and detailed than the later more stylized slick smooth surface of the previous fish sculpture. H. 11¾ in. (29.9 cm.) unsigned

1.168 **Latticino birds** Tall figures of birds, each with the body of clear glass internally decorated with rows of parallel diagonal filigree, with applied black legs and face, each mounted on a circular base. left H. 9¼ in. (23.5 cm.), center H. 16½ in. (41.9 cm.), rignt H. 13½ in. (34.3 cm.) unsigned

1.169 **Latticino bird detail**

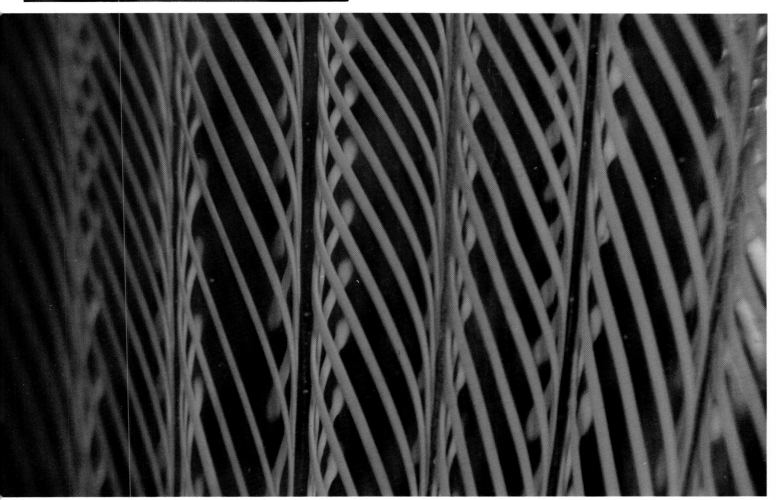

1.170 **Sommerso birds** Birds of thick clear glass, the left cased over black and silver leaf texture, and the right of silver leaf, each with black beak and eyes. L. 8 in. (20.3 cm.) H. 6¼ in. (15.9 cm.) unsigned

1.171 **Bullicante paperweight pear** Paperweight in the form of a pear in hollow green glass encased in thick clear glass in sommerso technique, with regularly placed air bubbles, and applied green stem and leaf. H. 6⅜ in. (16.2 cm.) paper label GENUINE VENETIAN GLASS MADE IN MURANO ITALY

1.172 **Cenedese sommerso apple** Clear glass paperweight in the form of an apple with encased gold metallic form in the center and applied clear stem and leaf. D. 3 in. (7.6 cm.) engraved signature CENEDESE, foil label MURANO CENEDESE VETRI, and paper label CENEDESE GLASS MURANO MADE IN ITALY

1.173 **Pear and apple paperweights** Opaque yellow glass paperweights in the form of a pear and an apple each with an applied cloudy white stem and leaf, the base and one side sliced and ground smooth in order to stand each one upright or on its side. H. 5¾ in. (14.6 cm.) unsigned

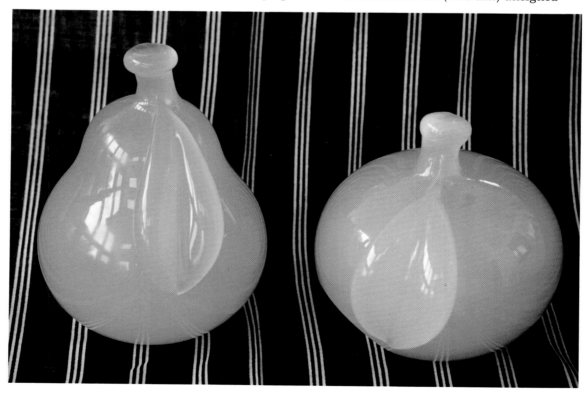

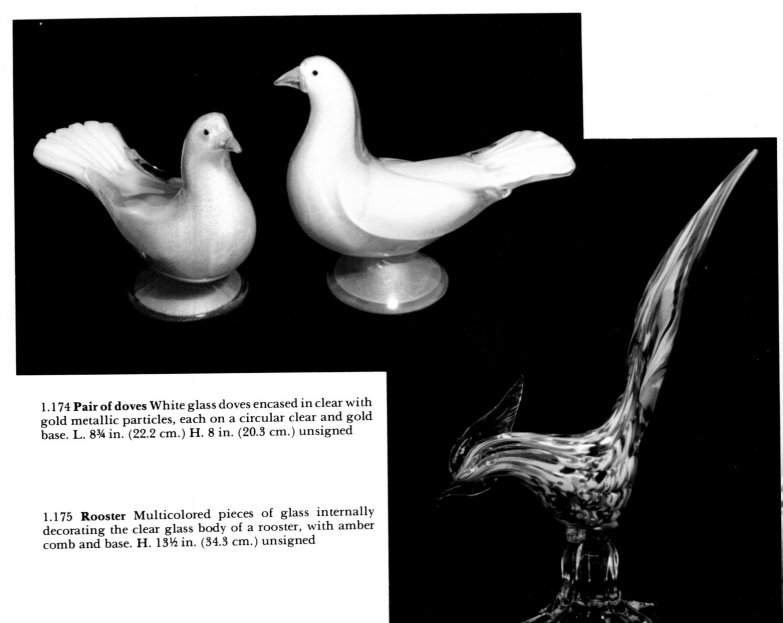

1.174 Pair of doves White glass doves encased in clear with gold metallic particles, each on a circular clear and gold base. L. 8¾ in. (22.2 cm.) H. 8 in. (20.3 cm.) unsigned

1.175 Rooster Multicolored pieces of glass internally decorating the clear glass body of a rooster, with amber comb and base. H. 13½ in. (34.3 cm.) unsigned

1.176 Birds Two turquoise and white opalescent glass birds with short pointed tails, and a bright yellow bird with its head turned around to face its long feathered tail. turquoise L. 5¼ in. (13.3 cm.) yellow L. 3⅞ in. (9.8 cm.) unsigned

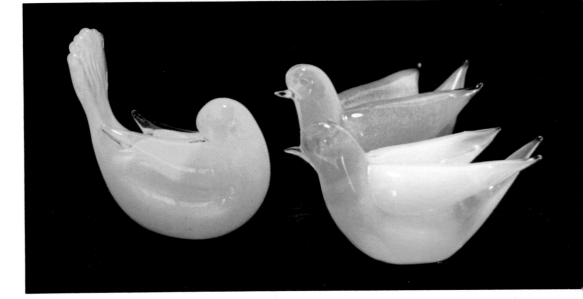

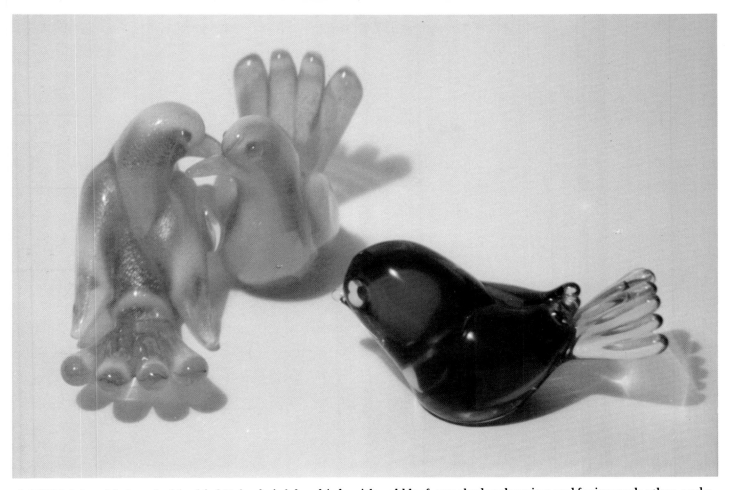

1.177 Pink lovebirds and a bluebird Pair of pink lovebirds with gold leaf, attached at the wing and facing each other, and a bluebird with similar feathered tail. pink L. 5 in. (12.7 cm.) blue L. 3¼ in. (8.3 cm.) pink, unsigned but probably by Seguso; blue, with paper label SEGUSO VETRI D'ARTE MURANO MADE IN ITALY

1.178 Two pairs of birds Pair of clear glass doves internally decorated with air bubbles, gold metallic particles, and teal green; a pair of pink glass birds shaded to clear glass feathered tails, with metallic particles. green L. 5 in. (12.7 cm.) pink L. 5 in. (12.7 cm) unsigned but possibly by Seguso

1.179 **Two ducks** Pink glass duck with gold particles and a clear glass beak and feet; a clear glass duck with face turned to the side and standing on a rocky base, internally decorated with gold particles and teal green. pink H. 6¼ in. (15.9 cm.) green H. 6¼ in. (15.9 cm.) pink unsigned and green with paper label MADE IN ITALY and probably by Seguso

1.180 **Barbini standing ducks** Amethyst sommerso duck in clear cristallo with applied clear and gold foil feet and beak, with another of opaque orange encased in clear glass with gold leaf inclusions and applied feet and beak. H. 6 in. (15.2 cm.) H 9¼ in. (23.5 cm.) unsigned

1.181 **Duck on a bowl** Teal green duck with gold leaf, standing on an amber and green bowl folded inward. D. 7½ in. (19 cm.) H. 6 in. (15.2 cm.) unsigned but probably by Barbini

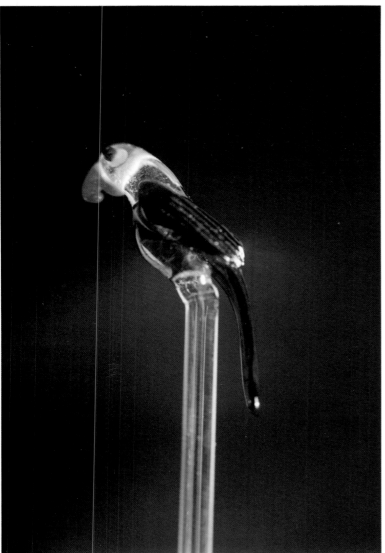

1.182 **Parrot drink stirrer** Red, white, and blue glass parrot mounted on a glass straw. These whimsical lampwork animals and other figures were made in Italy as well as Germany, Austria, and Czechlovakia. bird L. 1½ in. (3.8 cm.) unsigned

1.183 Vistosi bird designed by Paolo Pianon Blue-gray glass bird with inclusions of green and turquoise murrhine, a slice of cane for each eye, and mounted on copper wire legs. This series of comical birds on wire legs is one of Vistosi's most successful designs and easily identifiable even if unsigned. H. 10⅛ in. (25.7 cm.) unsigned. *Background courtesy groundworks unlimited.*

1.184 Salviati flower candleholders Lattimo flower petals sprinkled with gold leaf, surrounding clear glass candleholders, and mounted on clear leaves with gold leaf. H. 3½ in. (8.9 cm.) paper label SALVIATI & CO. VENICE MADE IN ITALY

1.185 **Salviati abstract sculpture** Three part abstract sculpture of a smoke gray smooth glass disc mounted between a clear glass disc and rectangular base chiseled and cut to resemble ice. H. 11 in. (27.9 cm.) L. 9½ in. (24.1 cm.) engraved SALVIATI VENEZIA 168/500

CHAPTER II

Scandinavia

As with any field, from architecture to fashion, the simpler the design the fewer opportunities there will be to disguise mistakes. Good unimbelished designs challenge both designers and artisans. While ornaments, trim, and pattern add interest, they also provide wider margins for error underneath. In order to be effective, simple designs must be perfectly proportioned and executed. Colorless glass must be flawlessly clear; bubble or teardrop shaped vessels must be graceful and true to the medium —reminders that the glass was once hot and liquid.

Scandinavian glassmakers have continually accepted the challenge of producing simple, elegant designs. With exceptions such as Palmqvist's Ravenna technique, with its bold color and overall pattern, Scandinavian color has been used with restraint. The glass is, therefore, rarely confused with Italian, which depends so much on vibrant color and complexity for its success. Where Murano artists explored and perfected colorful techniques using filigree, canes, mosiac, and metallic powders, Swedish artists invented less flamboyant Graal, Ariel, Kraka, and Ravenna, and in Finland and Denmark color was more often spare or absent. The following examples, from cool, icy, minimal forms to modernist paintings within glass, should indicate the range of Scandinavian fifties glass and some of the points between.

2.1 **Orrefors Ariel vase, "The Girl and the Dove" designed by Edvin Ohrström** Heavy walled crystal vase of ovoid form with tapering top and wavey opening, the clear glass internally decorated in the Ariel technique in amber and deep blue; the design "Flickan and Duvan" (The Girl and the Dove) was introduced in 1937. H. 7½ in. (19cm.) engraved signature *Photo courtesy of Orrefors*

110

2.2 **Orrefors Ariel vase "The Gondolier" designed by Edvin Ohrström** Thick walled cylindrical vase with clear base and body internally decorated in the Ariel technique in shades of blue and amber; the design was introduced by Ohrström in 1946. H. 6¾ in. (17 cm.) engraved signature *Photo courtesy of Orrefors*

2.3 **Detail of "The Gondolier"** *Photo courtesy of Orrefors*

2.4 Orrefors Ariel bowl designed by Edvin Ohrström Clear
crystal bowl with blue abstract cat, plants, stripes, and
dots in Ariel technique. D. 7 in. (17.8 cm.) engraved
signature E OHRSTROM ORREFORS SWEDEN
ARIEL NR. 434 *Courtesy of Ralph & Terry Kovel*

2.5 Orrefors Graal vase designed by Edward Hald Thick
clear crystal with purple parallel vertical stripes in Graal
technique, with an applied heavy clear crystal base, made
in 1953. H. 8½ in. (21.6 cm.) engraved signature
ORREFORS SWEDEN S. GRAAL 1311 EDWARD
HALD. *Background courtesy Brunschwig and Fils.*

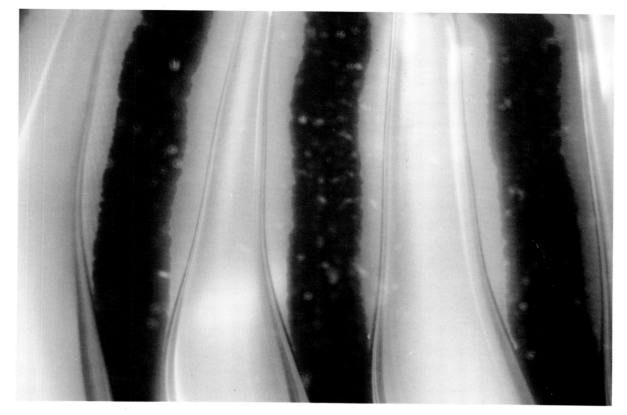

2.6 **Ariel detail**

2.7 **Orrefors Ariel bowl designed by Edvin Ohrström** Elongated trapped air bubbles of turquoise and black in the clear glass in the Ariel technique, done in 1952. D. 4⅜ in. (11.1 cm.) engraved signature ORREFORS ARIEL NO. 1711E EDVIN OHRSTROM

2.8 Orrefors "Fishgraal" vases designed by Edward Hald
Originally designed by Hald in 1945, the popular
Fishgraal has been produced in limited quantities ever
since. The motif of fish swimming in seaweed is almost
always in vivid greens using the Graal technique in clear
thick-walled crystal, but occasionally the design is in
black. Although the theme is the same, no two are exactly
alike, as illustrated in these examples. left H. 5⅜ in. (13.7
cm.) produced in 1973 with engraved signature
ORREFORS GRAAL NR. 236-E. 3 *Collection of Michael
Joseph Antiques, Cleveland;* right H. 4⅞ in. (12.4 cm.)
produced in 1962 with engraved signature ORREFORS
GRAAL NR. 234 S EDWARD HALD

Opposite page:

2.9 Orrefors Kraka vases designed by Sven Palmqvist
Elongated and slightly bulbous cylindrical vase, heavy
teardrop vase, and short cylindrical and slightly bulbous
vase, each with a clear crystal base and of clear crystal
internally decorated in the Kraka or fishnet pattern, in
which a blue net surrounds amber diamonds, each with a
single trapped air bubble, designed by Palmqvist in 1954.
left H. 13 in. (33 cm.), center H. 8¼ in. (21 cm.), right H. 8⅝
in. (22 cm.) engraved signatures *Photo courtesy of Orrefors*

2.10 **Orrefors Ravenna bowl designed by Sven Palmqvist** The Ravenna technique uses a layer of colored glass designed with a pattern, which is then filled with a different color, and covered with another layer of glass. In this bowl, the blue glass is decorated with a red textured framework of squares, designed in 1949. W. 9 in. (23 cm.) H. 5⅞ in. (15 cm.) engraved signature *Photo courtesy of Orrefors*

2.11 **Orrefors Ravenna bowl designed by Sven Palmqvist** Blue bowl with regular little windows of red and clear texture, designed by Palmqvist in 1949. W. 12¼ in. (31 cm.) H. 4⅜ in. (11 cm.) engraved signature *Photo courtesy of Orrefors*

2.12 **Nuutajärvi-Notsjö vase designed by Kaj Franck** Amber encased in thick clear crystal and cut in a flattened four-sided vase tapering to a narrower base, designed by Franck in 1963. H. 6¼ in. (16.5 cm.) paper label NUUTAJARVI NOTSJO 1793 SUOMI FINLAND and engraved signature K. FRANCK. NUUTAJARVI NOTSJO 63

2.13 **Kosta hexagonal vase** Green encased in thick clear crystal, the clear base with one large trapped air bubble, the vase cut with six sides tapering to a narrower base. H. 7⅝ in. (19.5 cm.) engraved KOSTA I 2457

2.14 **Two Swedish sommerso vases** Heavy clear crystal encasing a droplet shaped center, the left in amber, probably by Gerda Strömberg, who worked for Strömbergshyttan until 1955; the right in cobalt blue designed by Vicke Lindstrand in the early 1960s for Kosta. left H. 12¾ in. (32.4 cm) engraved S T R O M B E R G 3986; right H. 7 in. (17.8 cm.) engraved LH 1826 *Courtesy of Ralph and Terry Kovel*

2.15 **Kosta striped vase designed by Vicke Lindstrand** Turquoise interior asymmetrically placed in thick clear crystal casing, internally decorated with thin dark brown wavy stripes, made in 1962. H. 9¼ in. (23.5 cm.) paper label with crown KOSTA SWEDEN and engraved KOSTA LH 1719 *Courtesy of Ralph and Terry Kovel*

2.17 **Kosta circular bowl** Low round bowl of clear crystal internally decorated with cobalt blue and green curving stripes in varying thickness. D. 4½ in. (11.4 cm.) cellophane label KOSTA SWEDEN and engraved signature KOSTA 76776 and indecipherable name beginning with W

2.16 **Kosta vase designed by Vicke Lindstrand** Flattened vase flaring at the top, of pink glass internally decorated with parallel vertical white stripes, on a clear crystal base, designed by Lindstrand and pictured in the 1955/56 catalog. H. 3¼ in. (8.3 cm.) W. 4⅜ in. (11.1 cm.) engraved LH 1058

2.18 **Two Flygsfors biomorphic bowls designed by Paul Kedelv** Amoeboid three-lobed blobs are among the most typical fifties forms, and Paul Kedelv frequently used them. These bowls are in amber, gold, and clear glass with a thin opaque white stripe near the rim between the gold and clear. average D. 7¾ in. (19.7 cm.) engraved signature **FLYGSFORS 55 KEDELV**

2.19 **Two Åfors biomorphic bowls** Small bowl of clear crystal encasing typical fifties colors, hot pink and chartreuse, in four-lobed biomorphic shapes. Largest D. 4½ in. (11.4 cm.) pink engraved AFORS 2007 RUBIN, chartreuse engraved AFORS 2007 GHARL?

2.20 **Skruf bowl designed by Bengt Edenfalk** Circular bowl of clear crystal with inclusions of green, black, and amber bits of glass and trapped air bubbles near the base, designed in 1973 but in the spirit of the 50s. D. 5¾ in. (14.6 cm.) acid stamp SCRUF SWEDEN and engraved signature **BENGT EDENFALK 73**

2.21 **Kastrup Holmegaard bottle-vases** Two cased -vivid red over opaque white and maroon over white —and one of opaque yellow, the symmetrical cylindrical bottles each with a narrow cylindrical neck and perpendicular lip. These 1960s pieces are quite a departure from the colorless Holmegaard glass of the 50s. H. 9⅞ in. (25.1 cm), red H. 11⅞ in. (30.2 cm.), yellow H. 12 in. (30.5 cm.) paper labels KASTRUP HOLMEGAARD MADE IN DENMARK BY APPOINTMENT TO H.M. THE KING

2.22 **Nuutajärvi-Notsjö goblet vase designed by Kaj Franck** Goblet shaped vase with hollow knopped stem and hollow foot in clear glass with applied stripes (like mezza filigrana) in red, yellow, and blue, and atypical of Franck's work, which is rarely this colorful. H. 6¾ in. (17.1 cm.) engraved signature KAJ FRANCK NUUTAJARVI NOTSJO

2.23 Holmegaard vase designed by Per Lütken Bulbous vase in transparent pale turquoise with asymmetrical double pulled lip, so typical of the 50s that the same model was used as the cover illustration of an important contempory exhibition catalog (Liege, 1958). H. 9⅞ in. (25.1 cm.) engraved HOLMEGAARD 1955 PL

2.24 Holmegaard biomorphic bowl designed by Per Lütken Transparent smokey gray glass in three-lobed organic shape popularized in the 50s. L. 8¾ in. (22.2 cm.) engraved signature HOLMEGAARD 1956 PL

2.25 **Holmegaard vase designed by Per Lütken** Transparent green glass vase of cylindrical shape with solid base. H. 9 in. (22.9 cm.) engraved HOLMEGAARD PL 18121

2.26 **Orrefors "Applet" (Apple) designed by Ingeborg Lundin** Free blown crystal sculpture of an apple, the transparent symmetrical globe with a short cylindrical stem, designed by Lundin in 1957. D. 14⅛ in. (36 cm.) engraved signature *Photo courtesy of Orrefors*

2.27 Karhula-Iittala "Savoy" vase designed by Alvar Aalto
Designed by Aalto in 1936 for a design competition at
Karhula glassworks, the Savoy took first prize and was
then exhibited at the 1937 Paris Exposition; it was
important in the development of the biomorpic shapes so
popular in the 50s. Savoy was produced by Karhula from
1937-1949 and by Iittala from 1954-55, and from 1962-73,
and is back in production today. This is a later example.
H. 6¼ in. (15.9 cm.) L. 7 in. (17.8 cm.) acid stamp on the
base (backwards so it can be read from the top) ALVAR
AALTO

2.28 Iittala vase designed by Timo Sarpeneva
Smoky gray bulging cylindrical vase with small
spout and heavy clear base. H. 9⅛ in. (23.2 cm.)
engraved signature TIMO SARPENEVA 405

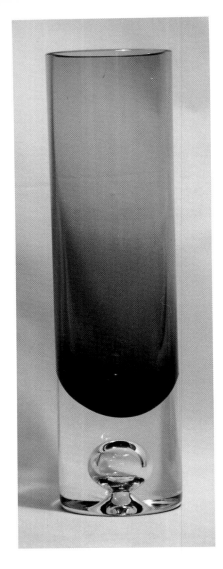

2.29 Iittala vase designed by Tapio Wirkkala Smoky blue cylindrical vase with thick clear base with a single large hollow bubble open to the base. H. 9⅜ in. (23.8 cm.) engraved signature TAPIO WIRKKALA 5586

2.30 Iittalo vase designed by Tapio Wirkkala Transparent armethyst cylindrical glass vase with clear base. H. 5 in. (12.7 cm.) engraved signature TAPIO WIRKKALA LA 358?

2.31 Iittala mushroom candleholders designed by Tapio Wirkkala Solid clear crystal symmetrical candleholders in Wirkkala's favored mushroom shape. H. 5¾ in. (14.6 cm.) engraved signature TAPIO WIRKKALA 3412

2.32 Iittala "Kanttarelli" (Chanterelle) vase designed by Tapio Wirkkala The chanterelle or mushroom vase was designed in 1947 by Wirkkala with a broad flared top, and it was produced by Iittala in a very limited edition of 50. From 1950-1960 a simpler version was produced in greater quantities, in varying sizes, with the same engraved vertical lines as the original model, but without the flaring top. It has since become one of the symbols of fifties Finnish glass. H. 4⅜ in. (11.1 m.) engraved signature TAPIO WIRKKALA IITTALA 55

2.33 Iittala "Kanttarelli" vases with leaf dishes designed by Tapio Wirkkala Pair of clear glass tapered vases with engraved parallel vertical lines, together with a pair of leaf-shaped dishes with engraved veining. vase H. 4⅜ in. (11.1 cm.) engraved TAPIO WIRKKALA IITTALA 55, dish L. 3½ in. (8.9 cm.) engraved T. WIRKKALA IITTALA

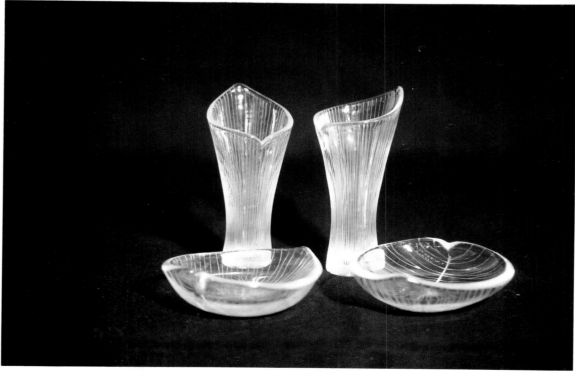

2.34 Iittala globe vase designed by Timo Sarpeneva
Round vase with tiny opening, the top half in charcoal gray and the bottom half in transparent pale gray. This series includes other sizes and symmetrical shapes, such as ovoid, (illustrated in Klein & Lloyd p. 252). H. 5¾ in. (14.6 cm.) engraved signature TIMO SARPENEVA IITTALA 57

2.35 Nuutajärvi-Notsjö bowl Thick clear glass bowl of flattened round form with internal layers of floating smoky design at the center. D. 6 in. (15.2 cm.) engraved NUUTAJARVI NOTSJO 53 and indecipherable artist signature

2.36 Hadeland vase designed by Herman Bongard
Rectangular flattened vase in white glass with regularly spaced trapped air bubbles, typical of Bongard's designs. W. 3 in. (7.6 cm.) engraved HADELAND 55 HB

2.37 Kosta hourglass vase designed by Vicke Lindstrand Clear crystal vase with flared bowl and base and very narrow waist in the shape of an hourglass. H. 7¾ in. (19.7 cm.) D. 7½ in. (19 cm.) engraved KOSTA 51689? LINDSTRAND

2.38 Kosta vase designed by Vicke Lindstrand Thick clear crystal vase in flattened cylindrical form with one side higher than the other, with an engraved squirrel. H. 4½ in. (11.4 cm.) engraved KOSTA LINDSTRAND 41376?

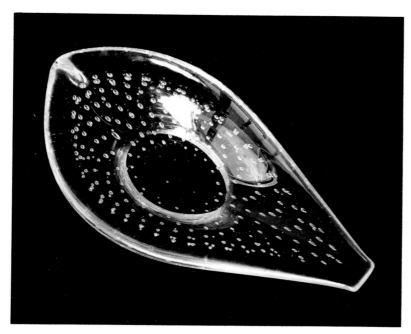

2.39 Kosta dish designed by Vicke Lindstrand Clear crystal dish in organic shape with regularly placed air bubbles, and in the 1958/59 catalog. L. 6⅜ in. (16.2 cm.) engraved KOSTA LH 1342

2.40 Flygsfors "Coquelle" vase designed by Paul Kedelv Organic shape with four stretched appendages, the milk glass center cased with brown and clear crystal, and one of the most fantastic sculptural forms of the "Coquelle" series, in which function is no longer taken seriously. H. 9⅝ in. (24.4 cm.) engraved **COQUELLE FLYGSFORS** 63

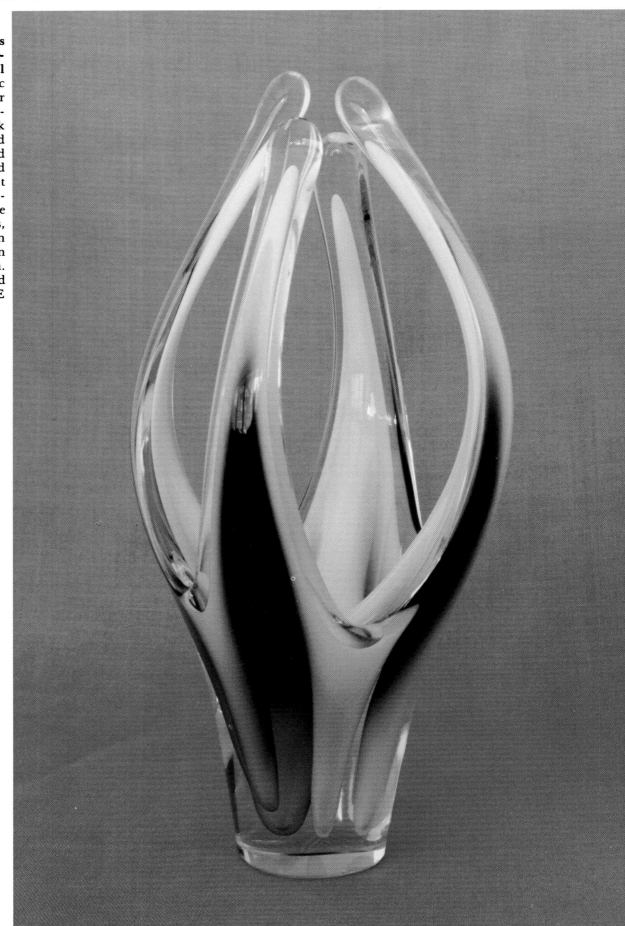

2.41 **Flygsfors "Coquelle" bowl designed by Paul Kedelv** Asymmetrical amoeboid or manta ray shape in milk glass and deep purple encased in clear crystal, with a central divider ending in a twisted tail, a truly fifties sculptural form. L. 7½ in. (19 cm.) engraved FLYGSFORS 55 KEDELV

2.42 **Flygsfors "Coquelle" bowl designed by Paul Kedelv** Milk glass encased with raspberry pink and then with clear crystal in sweeping biomorphic shape so typical of this series. L. 11½ in. (29.2 cm.) H 7 in. (17.8 cm.) engraved FLYGSFORS 57 COQUELLE

2.43 **Iittala "Orkidea" (Orchid) vase designed by Timo Sarpeneva** No longer with even an implied function, this droplet shaped sculpture has a bubble opening to the surface, a reminder that these forms were once hollow enough to be vessels. The "Orchid" series, made in varying heights, was designed in 1954 and won the Grand Prix at the Milan Triennale that year. H. 6 in. (15. 2 cm.) engraved signature TIMO SARPENEVA 3568?

2.44 **Hollow birds** Blue and teal green interior encased in clear glass in the shape of stylized birds. H. 4 in. (10.2 cm.) unsigned, but probably Swedish

2.45 **Kosta cat designed by Vicke Lindstrand** Amber glass sculpture of a seated cat with cut and unpolished spots. H. 8 in. (20.3 cm.) cellophane label with crown and KOSTA SWEDEN and engraved KOSTA LG 5736

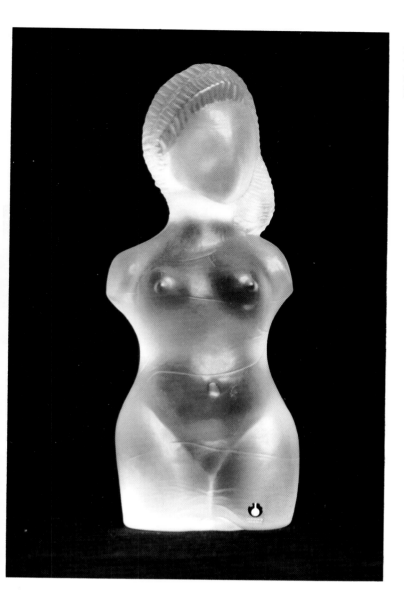

2.46 Pukeberg female figure designed by Westerberg
Frosted glass female torso with featureless face. H. 7¾ in.
(19.7 cm.) label PUKEBERG SWEDEN and cellophane
label DESIGN UNO WESTERBERG

2.47 Riihimäki duck Comical stylized duck with purple
glass solid cylindrical body, clear ball for a head, purple
hat, and applied milk glass beak. H. 5¾ in. (14.6 cm.)
paper label KUMELA RIIHIMAKI MADE IN FINLAND
and engraved KUMELA A. COLEMA?

CHAPTER III

Other Countries

In 1959 the Corning Museum of Glass held an exhibition of contemporary glass and produced an important catalog presenting glass from twenty-three countries. Besides Italy and Scandinavia, countries such as Czechoslovakia, England, Germany, and the United States were well-represented. But the 1950s were not the most significant years for glass design in these or other countries. Indeed, there were fine artists and examples of their work, but nothing comparable to the scale of activity taking place in Italy or Scandinavia. Two American companies specializing in blown and mold-blown tableware, Blenko and Erickson, are included here because, although they cannot be compared to the Murano companies, the spirit of fifties glass did touch them. Even production pieces shared the vibrant color, the shapes, and occasionally some of the internal decoration distinc-

tive of leading fifties glass. The Bimini Werkstätte examples are included, because they resemble fifties Murano glass and can be easily mistaken for it. Produced in the 1920s, the bold color and witty design seems to anticipate fifties tastes.

The intent of this chapter is to acknowledge that other artists and countries did participate in the fifties phenomenon more than it is to suggest that specific pieces are more worthy of attention or more typical than others. The decision to include one piece rather than another is arbitrary as the title "other countries" implies. It is hoped that readers will accept this and enjoy the representative pieces for what they are rather than for what they are not. As collectors and connoisseurs expand this field by contributing both information and objects, this little chapter will be seen for what it is —a beginning.

Erickson Freehand Glass

Bremen, Ohio   1943-1961

in Color

by
Ramona C. and Franklin H. Knower

HANDMADE by Erickson

3.1 **Erickson Freehand Glass** Book cover with 8 examples of vases: the two on the bottom right have the distinctive Erickson paperweight base with air bubbles, and the bottom center is in the style of Vicke Lindstrand, not surprising, since Carl Erickson was a Swedish-born glass artist who brought the spirit of Swedish design to his Ohio factory.

135

3.2 Erickson vases in green 19 examples of Erickson glass including bullicante (bubbled), two-toned, and folded in the Murano manner.

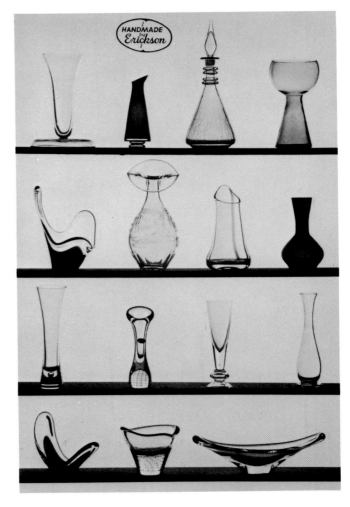

3.3 Erickson vases and bowls 15 examples of Erickson glass including three bowls in the style of Flygsfors' "Coquelle" series.

3.4 **Erickson glass bowls** 12 Erickson bowls, the top row in amoeboid shapes similar to the Flygsfors "Coquelle" series, the middle two in the second row with air bubbles similar to Pairpoint, where Carl Erickson worked before starting his own company.

3.5 **Erickson green bullicante bowl** Symmetrical round bowl on narrow foot in green glass internally decorated with regularly placed air bubbles. D. 11 in. (27.9 cm.) *Collection of Anita Singer*

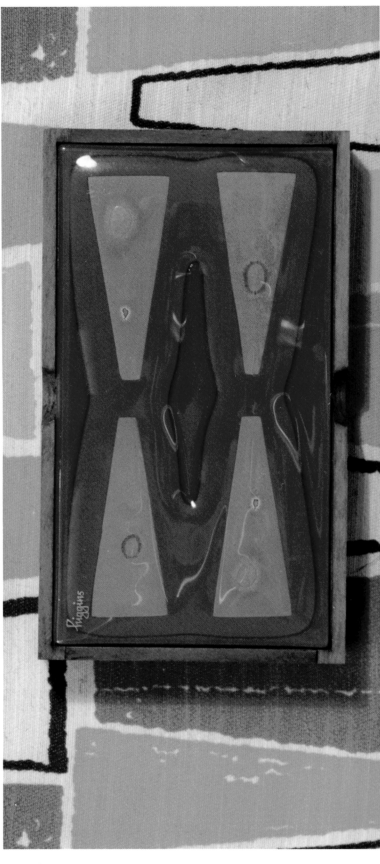

3.6 **Higgins ashtray** Molded glass with orange and gray enameled geometric design, designed by Michael Higgins. L. 7 in. (17.8 cm.) W. 5 in. (12.7 cm.) gold enamel signature HIGGINS

3.7 **Higgins cigarette box** Wood box with molded and glass cover in orange with gray and deep orange enameled geometric design, by Michael Higgins. L. 7½ in. (19 cm.) W. 4½ in. (11.4 cm.) gold enamel signature HIGGINS

3.8 Blenko bottle with stopper Orange shaded to yellow-orange glass bottle of symmetrical tapered form with orange teardrop stopper. H. 15½ in. (39.4 cm.) unsigned, but probably Blenko, though the same design was made by Vetreria Etrusca in Murano (illustrated in Neuwirth 232)

3.9 Blenko tumblers Clear tumblers with applied ruby red spiral (also made in sea green, amethyst, sky blue, and turquoise) and pictured in the Blenko catalog no. 600HB. H. 6¾ in. (17.1 cm.) Double hiball of the same design is 8½ in. unsigned

3.10 **Steuben crystal vase** Clear crystal flared cylindrical vase engraved **NIREB** 1951, on a solid base with canted corners. H. 7⅝ in. (19.4 cm.) engraved STEUBEN *Courtesy of Michael Joseph Antiques, Cleveland*

3.11 **Steuben crystal ashtrays** Pair of thick clear crystal astrays, each of round form with applied cigarette rests. D. 5⅝ in. (14.3 cm.) engraved STEUBEN

3.12 Steuben bouquet vase, creamer, and sugar Waisted bouquet vase with flared top designed by George Thompson in 1951 (#8020) H. 6½ in. (16.5 cm.) D. 9½ in. (24.1 cm.); cream pitcher with solid applied handle designed by Irene Benton in 1947 (#7941) W. 5¼ in. (13.3 cm.); sugar bowl with two symmetrical applied handles designed by Irene Benton in 1947 (#7942) W. 5¾ in. (14.6 cm.) each engraved STEUBEN *Collection of Valerie Pollak*

3.13 Steuben bowl Crystal bowl with three-sided base. D. 10 in. (25.4 cm.) engraved STEUBEN *Collection of Valerie Pollak*

3.14 Steuben flared teardrop candlesticks Pair of symmetrical candlesticks, each with a trapped air bubble in the base, designed by Donald Pollard in 1952 (#8032) H. 5 in. D. 5 in. (12.7 cm.) engraved STEUBEN *Collection of Valerie Pollak*

3.15 **Daum crystal vase** Thick walled crystal with four ribs, two flaring out as extensions of the top in a characteristically fifties shape. H. 8½ in.(21.6 cm.) engraved DAUM FRANCE *Collection of Dr. & Mrs. Albert Bennett*

3.16 **Daum crystal bowl** Heavy sculptural bowl of clear crystal in varying thickness. H. 3⅝ in. (9.3 cm.) D. 7¼ in. (18.4 cm.) engraved DAUM NANCY

3.17 Chalet handkerchief vase Ruffled adaptation of Murano fazzoletto in raspberry shaded to pale pink by Chalet Artistic Glass Ltd. of Cornwall, Ontario, Canada. Although made in the 60s (the company operated from 1962-1980), the vase definitely has a fifties look. H. 9 in. (22.9 cm.) acid stamp CHALET CANADA

3.18 Chinese cased vases Clear glass cased over vibrant red, over milk glass interiors, the symmetrical vases each with broad shoulders tapering to narrower base, narrow neck with flared lip, and applied clear handles. H. 8¼ in. (21 cm.) foil label SNOWFLAKES MADE IN CHINA

3.19 Striped vase, possibly by Leerdam Flattened symmetrical vase with wide shoulders of clear glass with blue and green wide spiraling stripes, possibly designed by Floris Meydam for Leerdam. H. 7¾ in. (19.7 cm.) unsigned

3.20 Maltese sommerso vase by Mdina Glass Flattened round vase with narrow neck of thick clear glass internally decorated with blue, turquoise, and amber in an abstract pattern, and with large facets on one surface. H. 8½ in. (21.6 cm.) engraved MALTA MDINA and with artist's signature *Collection of Mervin and Sylvia Glickman*

3.21 Bimini Werkstätte cocktail glasses Featherweight clear glass, each internally decorated with a different color spiral stripe, with twisted stem and circular foot of black spirals. Although made in Austria in the 1920s, these Art Deco glasses have often been mistaken for 1950s Italian because of the colorful stripes and modern style. H. 5⅝ in. (14.4 cm.) unsigned

3.22 Bimini footed tumblers Featherweight glasses tapering to a circular black foot, each of clear glass with a single color spiral and wavey stripe in the Venetian style. H. 6⅛ in. (15.6 cm.) unsigned

3.23 **Bimini vases and bowls** Pair of tiny featherweight vases, each with three clear solid ball feet, together with a pair of short circular bowls, all in clear and red mezza filigrana in the Venetian style, but made in Austria in the 1920s. vase H. 2½ in. (6.3 cm.) bowl D. 2⅝ in. (6.8 cm.) unsigned

3.24 **Bimini mermaid glasses** Smoky gray featherweight glasses with white glass stems in the form of mermaids, easily mistaken for fifties Murano glass, but made in Austria in the 20s. H. 4 in. (10.2 cm.) unsigned

3.25 **Drink Stirrers** Miniature lampwork animals mounted on glass sticks. Average animal L. 1 in. (2.5 cm.) paper labels MADE IN CZECHOSLOVAKIA and MADE IN GERMANY

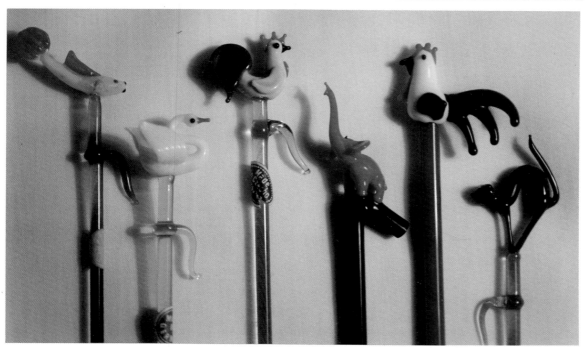

CHAPTER IV

Artists and Designers

In the scene from the movie *Back to the Future* where Michael J. Fox is transported back to the 1950s in a DeLorean, one of the characters assumes that his name is Calvin Klein because of the label on his jeans. In this day of designer labels we are so accustomed to products with names that anything else is generic and unfamiliar by comparison. When the designer label first appeared is unknown, but in the realm of glassmaking, the Art Nouveau years and then the postwar years of the 1950s stand out.

By the 50s, the major glass factories had hired full-time artistic directors to oversee and to design, not production pieces, but works of art that were routinely entered into international competitions, such as Milan Triennales and Venice Biennales. This arrangement bestowed notoriety on both the designer and the company. The following selected list includes names and statistics of individuals who made significant contributions in glassmaking during the 1950s. Much of the information regarding dates and places is from Beard, Deboni and Cocchi, Eidelberg, Grover, and Opie, where more details about individuals and companies can be found. Minor discrepencies in some dates may be partly due to translating material from one language to another.

Display at XI Milan Triennale *Photo courtesy of © Domus (338:43, Jan. 1958)*

Barovier e Toso: vetri colorati.

Barovier & Toso vetri colorati at Venice Biennale
Photo courtesy of © Domus (323:26, Oct. 1956)

Jacob E. Bang 1899-1965,
Denmark Trained as an architect and sculptor at the Royal Danish Academy of Fine Arts in Copenhagen 1916-1921, Bang was a pioneer of Danish modern glass design in the 1930s. He was a designer at Holmegaard from 1925, art director from 1928-1942, and art director at Kastrup from 1957-1965. (Beard 216, Opie 151)

Alfredo Barbini b. 1912, Italy
A descendant of 17th-century glassmakers, Barbini began studying at tht age of ten at Abate Zanetti, the design school attached to the Murano Glass Museum. After apprenticing at S.A.I.A.R. Ferro-Toso, and earning the title of maestro at the Cristalleria di Murano, working for Zecchin and Martinuzzi begining in 1932, working briefly with Seguso Vetri d'Arte, and serving as art director for Gino Cenedese (company began in 1946), he began his own workshop in 1950. Barbini is noted for the use of heavy

glass sculpture and thick-walled vessels, and was responsible for new techniques of internal decoration such as "vetro fumato." He has won several international awards, including Croce di Cavaliere al Merito in 1955. His son Flavio joined in the 60s, and they are active today. (Barbini company brochure, Deboni & Cocchi 113, Grover 132-34)

Angelo Barovier b. 1927, Italy
The son of Ercole, Angelo is a painter and a glass designer. After studying at the Universities of Padua and Ferrara, he earned a doctorate in law. He joined Barovier and Toso in 1947 and developed new series which were exhibited at Milan Triennales and Venice Biennales. Angelo became export manager of the firm and has been managing director since 1974. He was also Vice President of the Venetian Indus-

trialists and is now national President of the Italian Art Glass Industry. (Dr. Angelo Barovier)

Ercole Barovier 1889-1974 Italy
A descendant of Angelo Barovier, the renowned 15th-century artist and glassmaker who is credited with perfecting Venetian "cristallo" and "calcedonio" glass, Ercole Barovier was an artist and a chemist. He joined the family glass business with his brother Nicolò in 1919 when Artisti Barovier became Vetreria Artistica Barovier & C. In 1933 he was the sole owner of the factory, and in 1936 he founded a glass factory with another old company, Ferro Toso. The managers of Ferro Toso, Artemio and Decio Toso, were from a family that had been in the glass business since the 17th century. The new company, called Ferro-Toso Barovier, changed to Barovier &

Dr. Angelo Barovier and his son Jacopo *Photo ©Michele Gregolin, courtesy of Angelo Barovier/Barovier & Toso*

Toso & C. in 1939, and Barovier & Toso in 1942, which is the current name. Barovier developed new colors and technical processes. During his long career as president and artistic director (until 1972) he created thousands of models of art glass and won numerous prizes and awards. His most significant contribution is with murrhine glass beginning in 1948 and blossoming during the 50s. (Dr Angelo Barovier, Beard 217, Deboni & Cocchi 114, Dorigato 150-51)

Fulvio Bianconi b. 1915, Italy
As a young man, Bianconi designed glass for Madonna dell'Orto in Venice. After designing for Cenedese and Vistosi, he met Venini in 1948. His "fazzoletto" design soon became a symbol for Venini, and he stayed with the company until 1951, the year that he exhibited at the Milan Triennale. Bianconi free-lanced for various firms including Venini. His notable designs included "commedia dell'arte" and other figures, further development of the fazzoletto vase, vessels in biomorphic shapes, and plaids. After working for Vistosi in the early 1960s and winning awards at Milan Trienalles in 1963 and 1964, he returned to Venini in 1966. Bianconi has worked independently with several furnaces in Murano and in Switzerland in 1980. (Deboni & Cocchi 114, Eidelberg 363)

Ercole Barovier *Photo courtesy of Angelo Barovier/Barovier & Toso*

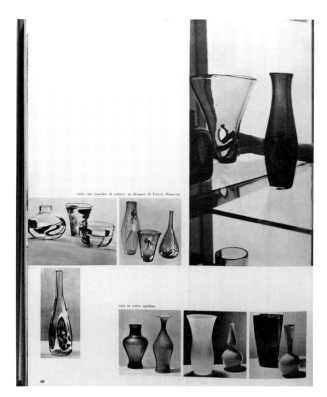

Fulvio Bianconi designs for Venini *Photo courtesy of* ©*Domus (361:36, Dec. 1959)*

William John Blenko 1854-1933, England
Blenko was an apprentice at a bottle factory at the age of 10 and went to school at night to learn chemistry (to color glass) and French (the language of medieval glass treatises). After learning the art of mouthblown stained glassmaking, he came to the United States and made his first attempt at opening a glass factory. Bad luck caused several false starts, until Blenko Glass in Milton, West Virginia finally became succesful in the 1920s after Blenko's son William H. joined him. Although William senior did not live to see his company blossom in the 1950s, he had laid the foundation. (Eige & Wilson 5-15)

Herman Bongard b.1921, Norway
After receiving an education at the National School of Crafts and Industrial Design in Oslo, Bongard joined Hadeland as a designer in 1947. He is noted for his broad flat forms in glass and also worked in pottery, silver, and wood. (Polak 72)

Tomaso Buzzi 1900-1981 Italy
After studying architecture and design at del Politecnico di Milano, Buzzi earned a Ph.D. in 1923. In 1924 he opened a modern interior design studio called Il Labirinto. After developing a friendship with Venini, Buzzi met Napoleone Martinuzzi, and in 1932, through Buzzi, Martinuzzi became acquainted with the Venini style. Buzzi held the highest position at the school of architecture in Milan, as director from 1930-1954. He was involved with both the design and implementation of glass for Venini, and developed the series "Alga & Laguna." (Deboni & Cocchi 115)

Gino Cenedese 1907-1973, Italy
Cenedese began his own factory in 1946 and designed sculpture and vessels in abstract shapes with Alfredo Barbini until the end of 1950. He collaborated with sculptor Napoleone Martinuzzi and designer Fulvio Bianconi in the 50s, and creations included "azquari," big blocks of glass with inclusions of figures, which were sometimes abstract. From 1959 Antonio Da Ros was artistic director, and from 1964-1970 maestro Ermanno Nason collaborated with him at Cenedese. One of their accomplishments was the work with "sommersi" vessels in layers of graduated color. (Deboni & Cocchi 116)

Andries Copier b. 1901, the Netherlands
Copier studied at the School of Graphic Arts at Utrecht and the Academy of Art at Rotterdam 1917-1925. He began as an apprentice at Leerdam in 1914, as a glass designer in 1922, and began designing Unica pieces in 1924. He was artistic director at Leerdam from 1927-1971 and head of Unica Studio. Important exhibits and awards include a silver medal at the 1925 Paris Exposition, exhibits at the Leerdam Pavilion and a grand prize at the Brussels World Fair in 1958, and an award at the Milan Triennale in 1960. A co-founder of the Leerdam Glass School in 1940, Copier served as its first head. (Beard 221, Eidelberg 369)

Gunnar Cyrén b. 1931, Sweden
Trained at the National College of Art, Craft, and Design in Stockholm, Cyrén received diplomas in goldsmithing in 1951 and in silversmithing in 1956. He designed glass for Orrefors from 1959-1970, where he introduced opaque, vividly colored glass, then free-lanced from 1976. Cyrén won a Lunning Prize in 1966 and continued to work in silver and gold as well as glass. He was featured in recent editions of *Orrefors Gallery* as one of the leading Orrefors artists. (Beard 221, Eidelberg 369, Opie 153)

Bengt Edenfalk b. 1924, Sweden
After studying at the National College of Arts, Crafts, & Design in Stockholm from 1947-1952, Edenfalk was hired as the first full-time staff designer at Scruf, in 1953. He became art director and remained at Skruf until 1978. During that time he was successful in various competitions, such as Milan Triennales, and was a leading name in the 1959 Corning Glass Center exhibit. In 1978 he joined Kosta Boda and has recently been featured in special

company catalogs. (Grover 182, Kosta Boda 1990 19, Opie 154)

Carl Ebert Erickson 1889-1966, United States
Erickson was born in Sweden and learned glass-making from his father, Carl Oscar Erickson. He came to the United States as a teenager and attended Boston University while apprenticing at Pairpoint Glass in New Bedford, Massachusetts. After 20 years at Pairpoint from 1912-1932, he worked for Libbey Glass in Toledo, Ohio until 1936, followed by Blenko in Milton, West Virginia. Carl and his brother Steven started the Erickson Glassworks in Bremen, Ohio in 1943; Carl bought his brother's interest in 1953, and the company closed in 1961. (Knower 2-5)

Kaj Franck 1911-1989, Finland
Franck studied furniture design and interior design at the Central School of Industrial Design in Helsinki from 1929-1932, where he began teaching in 1945 and served as director from 1960-1968. At the same time, he was head of design at Arabia doing utility ware from 1945-1973 and art director from 1968-1973. He designed glass at Iittala from 1946-1950, at Nuutajärvi from 1950-1976, and served as Nuutajärvi art director from 1960. In addition to glass, he also designed textiles and ceramics. He won many major international awards and medals, including a gold medal in 1951, two diplomas in 1954, and both a grand prize and a gold in 1957 at the Milan Triennales, a Lunning Prize in 1955, and a Prins Eugen Medal in 1965. (Beard 225-26, Eidelberg 372-73, Opie 155)

Kaj Franck bottle designs for Notsjö *Photo courtesy of ©Domus (336:8, Nov. 1957)*

Kaj Franck and other Finnish designs *Photo courtesy of ©Domus (336:9, Nov. 1957)*

Anzolo Fuga b. 1914 Italy
Fuga earned a diploma from the Instituto d'Arte di Venezia with specializations in illustration, print-making, and art glass design. He met Guido Balsamo-Stella, who encouraged him to dedicate his talent solely to art glass. He opened a studio after the War and specialized in painting on glass. Then from 1955-1962, he collaborated with A.V.E.M. designing large abstract pieces, often decorating them with murrhine under the guidance of Luciano Ferro. Fuga also taught at the Abate Zanetti evening art school attached to the Murano Glass Museum, from which several of the greatest glass teachers have graduated. (Deboni & Cocchi 116)

Luciano Gaspari b.1913, Italy
Gaspari began teaching at the Academy of Fine Arts in Venice in 1941. He designed heavy sommerso glass for Salviati & Co., exhibited widely, and won the Enapi Prize at the 1959 Milan Triennale. (Beard 226)

Edward Hald 1883-1980, Sweden
After studying painting and architecture at the Technical Academy in Dresden from 1904-1906, Hald studied at the Artists Studio School in Copenhagen in 1907, and then painting with Henri Matisse in Paris. He joined Orrefors in 1917 and was managing director from 1933-1944. He followed this

with free-lance work for Orrefors from 1944 until the late 1970s. Together with designer Simon Gate (1883-1945) and glassblower Knut Bergqvist (1873-1953), Hald was one of the leaders of Swedish modernism. He also won international prizes, such as the grand prize at the Paris Exposition in 1925 and the Prins Eugen Medal in 1945. (Beard 227-28, Opie 156)

Edward Hald Fishgraal design for Orrefors

Frances Higgins b. 1912, United States
Frances Higgins earned a B.S. degree from Georgia College and an M.F.A. from the Institute of Design in Chicago. She operated a glassworks with her husband Michael from 1948-58 and then designed for the Dearborn Glass Company. (Grover 24-26)

Michael Higgins b. 1908 England, worked in United States
Michael Higgins studied at several colleges, including London Central School of Arts and Crafts. He came to the United States and eventually became head of the Visual Design department at the Institute of Design in Chicago, where he met Frances. Together they operated a glassworks from 1948-1958, then designed for the Dearborn Glass Company. They specialized in enameled design on sheet glass. (Grover 24-26)

Paul Kedelv b. 1917, Sweden
Kedelv worked for Orrefors in Sweden and Nuutajärvi -Notsjö in Finland before joining Flygsfors in Sweden in 1949. During the 1950s he designed fantastic biomorphic and other asymmetrically shaped pieces, notably the "Coquille" series, which made the transition from vessel to sculpture. (Beard 231)

Nils Landberg b.1907, Sweden
Landberg studied at the School of Arts and Crafts in Gothenburg from 1923-1925, the Orrefors engraving school from 1925-1927, and in France and Italy. As an engraver and then designer at Orrefors from 1927-1972, he exhibited at the Paris Exhibition in 1937 and the New York World's Fair in 1939, and won international awards and medals, such as a gold medal at the Milan Triennale in 1957. (Beard 223, Eidelberg 381, Opie 161)

Vicke Lindstrand (Victor Emanuel) 1904-1983, Sweden
After studying advertising at the School of Arts and Crafts in Gothenburg from 1924-1927, Lindstrand worked as an illustrator and cartoonist. He was a designer at Orrefors from 1928-1940, a designer at Upsala-Ekeby from 1936-1950, and the art director from 1942. He designed a window for the Swedish Pavilion at the Paris Exposition in 1937 and a glass fountain for the 1939 New York World's Fair. As Kosta art director from 1950-1973, he participated in all major exhibitions, including the Milan Triennales and World's Fairs. Unlike his colleagues, he did not win awards. Nevertheless, Lindstrand is one of the superstars and creative forces behind the success of Scandinavian fifties glass. (Beard 234, Eidelberg 383-84, Opie 162)

Ingeborg Lundin b. 1921, Sweden
After studying at the Swedish State School, Lundin designed glass at Orrefors from 1947-1971. She participated in international exhibitions and won awards, including the Lunning Prize in 1954 and a gold medal at the Milan Triennale in 1957. (Beard 235)

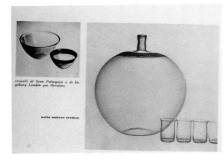

Ingeborg Lundin Apple and Sven Palmqvist bowls for Orrefors *Photo courtesy of ©Domus (336:6, Nov. 1957)*

Per Lütkin b. 1916, Denmark
Lütkin studied painting and technical drawing at

the School of Arts and Crafts in Copenhagen until 1937. He joined Kastrup Holmegaard as art director in 1942 where he has remained. His work has been in international exhibitions, such as Milan Triennales, and collected by museums from London to Corning, New York. (Beard 235, Opie 162)

Dino Martens 1894-1970, Italy
Martens studied painting and earned a diploma from the Accademia di Belle Arti di Venezia and initially worked as a painter. He then designed glass for S.A.L.I.R, Salviati, Cooperativa Mosaicisti Veneziana, and for Vetreria A. Toso before becoming artistic director for Aureliano Toso from 1938-1965. Martens worked with polychrome zanfirico and asymmetric patchwork and participated in international exhibitions. His famous "Oriente" and "Zanfirici" series have become symbols of 50s glass. (Beard 237, Deboni & Cocchi 116)

Dino Martens Oriente design for Aureliano Toso

Floris Meydam b. 1919, the Netherlands
Meydam joined Leerdam in 1935, where he later designed free-form spontaneous Unica glass. He began teaching at the Leerdam Glass School in 1944. (Beard 237)

Aldo Nason b. 1920, Italy
Son of Emilio Nason, he was one of the founders and a master glass artist at A.V.E.M. until founding his own glassworks.

Gunnar Nylund b.1904, France,
moved to Sweden After studying architecture with his father, Finnish portrait painter Felix Nylund,

Gunnar designed ceramics and glass for various companies including Bing and Grondahl and Rorstrand, where he was art director from 1930-1959. From 1954-1967 he was with Strömbergshyttan as a glass designer and art director. (Beard 239, Eidelberg 389-90, Opie 165)

Karl Edvin Ohrström b. 1906, Sweden
Ohrström studied at the National College of Art, Craft, and Design in Stockholm from 1925-1928, the Royal Swedish Academy of Art from 1928-1932, and studied drawing in Paris with Fernand Leger and others until 1934. He designed glass at Orrefors for two months each year from 1936-1958. He developed the Ariel technique, in which controlled air bubbles produce the design between layers of thick glass, with Vicke Lindstrand and Gustav Bergkvist in 1937. Major international exhibitions and awards include the 1937 Paris Exposition and 1939 New York World's Fair. (Beard 240, Eidelberg 390, Opie 165)

Sven Palmqvist 1906-1984, Sweden
Palmqvist studied at the Orrefors engraving school from 1928-1930, National College of Art, Craft, and Design in Stockholm from 1931-1933, the Royal Swedish Academy of Art in Stockholm from 1934-1936, and with Paul Connet in Paris from 1937-1939. He designed glass for Orrefors 1930-1972, where he developed the "Ravenna" and "Kraka" styles based on the Graal technique. Then from 1972-1984 he free-lanced at Orrefors. Major prizes include the grand prize at the Milan Triennale in 1957, grand prize at the Venice Biennale in 1976, and the Prins Eugen Medal in 1977. (Beard 241, Opie 166)

Flavio Poli 1900-1984, Italy
An interior decorator and ceramic artist, as well as a glass designer, Poli collaborated with I.V.A.M. of Giovita Vitali in 1929, and in 1934 joined Seguso-Barovier-Toso and designed the famous "Zodiaco" panel. In 1937 the company became Seguso Vetri d'Arte, and Poli became artistic director until 1963. From 1952-1963 he was best known for the sommerso technique. One of Italy's leading glass designers, Poli started his own factory in 1964 called Società Veneziana di Conterie e Cristellerie, but lasted only until 1966 due to ill health. His work is usually unsigned and has won awards including the grand prize at Milan Triennales in 1951, 1954, and 1960, the Compasso d'Oro in 1954, and a grand prize at the 1958 Brussels International Exposition. (Beard 242, Deboni & Cocci 118)

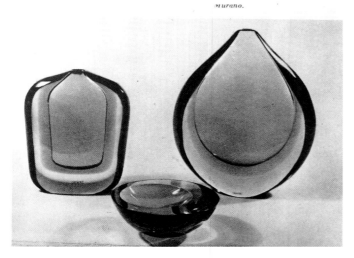

Flavio Poli designs for Seguso *Photo courtesy of ©Domus (323:27, Oct. 1956)*

Timo Sarpeneva b. 1926, Finland

After graduating from the Central School of Industrial Design in Helsinki in graphic design in 1948, Sarpeneva became a leading Finnish designer of ceramics, metal, wood, textiles, graphics, and plastic, in addition to glass. He designed glass for Iittala from 1950 as well as in other materials for numerous other companies. He has done installation designs for international exhibitions and his numerous major awards and medals include second prize at the Riihimäki glass competition in 1949, the Lunning Prize in 1956, grand prizes at Milan Triennales in 1954 and 1957, several gold and silver medals at Milan Triennales, and a gold medal from the Royal College of Art. (Beard 243-44, Eidelberg 397, Opie 169)

Timo Sarpeneva glass sculpture "Lansetti" (Lancet) Designed in 1952, the Lancet series won the Grand Prix at the Milan Triennale in 1954. *Photo courtesy of ©Domus (298:44, Sept. 1954)*

Carlo Scarpa 1906-1978, Italy

A graduate of the Accademia di Belle Arti di Venezia in 1926 and an important architect, Scarpa worked for Vetri Soffiati Muranesi Cappellin Venini & Co.

until 1925, Maestri Vetrai Muranesi Cappelin & C. until 1932, experimented with new color techniques and the application of gold and silver leaf, and rejoined Venini as artistic director in 1932. Scarpa is credited with Venini's revival of murrhine glass in 1938, and exhibited several murrhine designs in the 1940 Venice Biennale. He left in 1947, but may have continued to collaborate with Venini while devoting himself almost entirely to architecture. In 1951 Frank Lloyd Wright visited Murano and became influenced by Scarpa. (Deboni & Cocchi 119, Eidleberg 397-98)

Archimede Seguso b.1909, Italy

Born to a family that had been in the glass business since 1575, Seguso began at age 13 at Vetri Artistica Fratelli, where his father Antonio was one of ten partners. At age 20 he was the youngest master glassmaker in Murano. Together with his father and Antonio and Napoleone Barovier, he formed Seguso Vetri d'Arte in 1933 and made extremely avant garde massive glass sculpture. He left in 1942 and started his own company, Vetreria Archimede Seguso, in 1946. Latticino and delicate lacework are among his most important designs, and Seguso has exhibited widely and has won many international awards for designs such as "Merletto" in 1951, "Composizione lattimo" in 1954, and "Piume" in 1955. (Deboni & Cocchi 119, Eidelberg 398, Franzoi 13, 18, & 32)

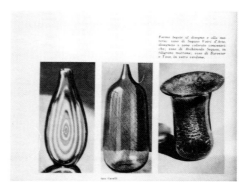

Archimede Seguso vaso filigrana (center) *Photo courtesy of ©Domus (298:53, Sept. 1954)*

R. S. Stennett-Wilson b. 1923 England

A designer of modern glass at Wedgwood Glass, Stennett-Wilson is the author of *The Beauty of Modern Glass*, London, 1958.

Ermanno Toso 1903-1973, Italy

The company Fratelli Toso was founded in 1854 by the five Toso brothers, and Ermanno Toso was artistic director from the 1930s. During the 1950s, he worked with colorful murrhine glass and filigree, but rarely signed pieces other than an occasional paper label.

Paolo Venini 1895-1959, Italy
A Milanese lawyer from a family of glassblowers, Venini formed a company in 1921 and incorporated in 1924 as Vetri Soffiati Muranesi Venini Cappellin & Co. The company is noted for the revival of filigrano techniques and has been the leading art glass producer in Italy. Venini oversaw the firm's operations and worked closely with some of the most important glass designers of the modern period. His genius helped to make the company's name synonamous with fifties Italian glass. (Beard 249)

Paolo Venini *Photo courtesy of ©Domus (361:31, Dec. 1959)*

Paolo Venini with a glass-blower *Photo courtesy of ©Domus (361:46, Dec. 1959)*

Paolo Venini and his glass *Photo courtesy of ©Domus (361:37, Dec. 1959)*

Tapio Wirkkala 1915-1985, Finland
Trained at the Central School of Industrial Design in Helsinki from 1933-1936, Wirkkala was the school's art director from 1951-1954. One of the most important postwar designers —industrial design, graphics, and ceramics, as well as glass —he worked for various companies, notably as artistic director of Iittala from 1946-1985, for Venini from 1959-1985, and with Raymond Loewy in the United States from 1955-1956. Wirkkala designed for international exhibitions between 1951 and 1971, such as the Finnish pavilions at Milan Triennales and the Brussels World's Fair in 1958. He has won numerous major international awards and medals, including the Lunning Prize in 1951, seven grand prizes at Milan Triennales, several gold and silver medals at Milan Triennales in 1951, 1954, 1960, and 1963, and the Prins Eugen Medal in 1980. (Beard 253, Eidelberg 40506, Opie 173)

Tapio Wirkkala designs *Photo courtesy of ©Domus (298:41, Sept. 1954)*

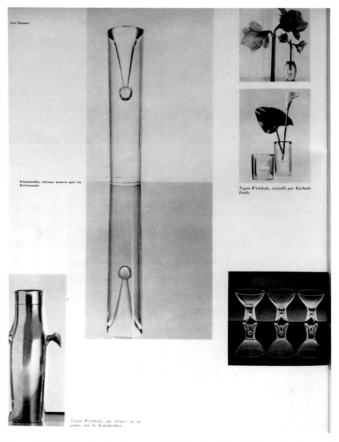

Tapio Wirkkala designs exhibited at the Milan Triennale
Photo courtesy of ©Domus (298:40, Sept. 1954)

CHAPTER V

Companies

Whether their roots were in Renaissance Italy or nineteenth-century Scandinavia, most of the following companies went through phases of modernization and change just prior to or during the 1950s. Hiring full-time artistic directors, sponsoring design competitions, and inviting fine artists in painting, sculpture, and architecture to join design staffs invigorated the companies and the art of glassmaking.

It was not uncommon for some of the most talented designers and glassmakers to work for several different glass furnaces, either consecutively or concurrently, particularly those who free-lanced. One explanation for the many stylistic similarities between art glass from different companies or even different countries was this sharing of the talent pool. Since so many of the members of this pool were also skilled in other artistic media, their designs connected glass with ceramics, metals, textiles, graphics, plastics, and even furniture and architecture. Training in fields apart from glass also brought in fresh perspectives. As Chris Hacker, vice president and design director at Steuben since 1987, aptly put it in a conversation with Kosta designer, Bertil Vallien, "Some of the best pieces we've developed in the last few years have been by previously non-glass designers, and I believe it's because they've been given the freedom of stupidity, if you will, or the lack of knowledge to try something that, you know, was so obviously not possible for the man who has been standing by the pot for many years." (*Glass* vol. 43 Spring 1991, p. 13) For example, Angelo Barovier, Hald, and Martens were first painters; Poli also worked in ceramics; Scarpa, Bang and Nylund were architects; Cyrén also worked in silver and gold; Franck also designed textiles, ceramics, and furniture; Nylund designed ceramics and glass for several companies; the two leading Finnish designers, Sarpeneva and Wirkkala, designed for a number of companies in every possible material, and Wirkkala even worked for Raymond Loewy in the United States and Venini in Murano. Barbini, Bianconi, Martens, and others each designed for several different Murano glassworks. In addition, companies frequently merged or took over one another, causing distinctions between them to become blurred.

Whether small but significant furnaces in Murano or a major glassworks in Sweden, these companies shared a common language in the art of glassmaking. Their designers met and exchanged ideas at international competitions, at World's Fairs, and sometimes at each other's glassworks. The resulting art glass is enormously varied yet oddly similar. Unintentionally or unconsciously, glass artists from different cultures and climates seemed to coordinate a great artistic effort. Whether "Kraka" at Orrefors or "reticello" at Venini, "Ravenna" or "murrine," the look is unmistakably fifties, and the following companies are to be credited with making it happen.

Åfors Glasbruk
Åfors was founded in 1876 in Smaland, Sweden by the brothers, and former glass craftsman from Kosta, Carl, Oskar, and Alfred Fagerland. Erik Åfors became manager in 1919, and in 1935 he purchased fifty per cent of Kosta. Åfors merged with Kosta in 1946. (Beard 209, Grover 155)

Aureliano Toso
The company was founded in 1910 in Murano by Aureliano Toso. Dino Martens was artistic director from 1938-1965. His work is distinguished by the use of filigree, canes, and aventurine (metallic particles) in patches or spontaneously scattered in the glass. The inclusion of irregularly-placed and brightly-colored threads and shapes resemble abstract paintings, not at all surprising since Martens was trained as a painter.

Arte Vetraria Muranese (A.V.E.M.)
A.V.E.M. was founded in 1932 in Murano by the master glassmakers who had left Succussori Andrea Rioda: Antonio, Egidio, Ottone, and Ulisse Ferro and Emilio Nasson. Giulio Radi became the company's only artistic director in 1935. Initially, they collaborated artistically with Vittorio Zecchin. The most important postwar work was innovative and colorful, designed by Radi and under the supervision of Aldo Nason. Luciano Ferro was a master glassblower who worked on firey and vibrant pieces designed by Anzolo Fuga, who free-lanced for A.V.E.M. from 1955-1962. They did not sign the pieces. Ada Ferro heads the company today. (Deboni & Cocchi 113, Heiremans cat. nos. 1-23, Sotheby's Nov. 10, 1990)

Barbini Glassworks
After working for S.A.I.A.R. Ferro Toso and other important Murano glass factories, Alfredo Barbini became a partner at Gino Cenedese & C. in 1947 and began his own furnace, Barbini Glassworks, in 1950. His son Flavio later assisted in designing glass, often in heavy sculptural forms. They won several international awards, such as the Croce di Cavaliere al merito in 1955. The company also made knicknacks, such as ashtrays and figurines, which were imported exclusively by Weil Ceramics & Glass Inc. in New York City with branches in Hingham, Massachusetts and Los Angeles.

Barovier & Toso
The company was founded in 1878 by Antonio Salviati but had origins in the 14th century in Murano. It went under the name Artisti Barovier at the end of the 19th century and then Vetreria Artistica Barovier in 1919. In 1936 Artemio and Decio Toso (owners of S.A.I.A.R. Ferro Toso) merged with Barovier to form Ferro-Toso-Barovier, which became Barovier & Toso in 1942. Their highest achievements were during the 1950s, especially with the imaginative and technically superior use of patchwork and murrhine. The textured surface of "Barbarico" is one of several designs unique to the company.

Ercole and Nicolò Barovier in the laboratory in 1924
Photo courtesy of Angelo Barovier/Barovier & Toso

158

Vetreria Artistica Barovier & C. in 1924 *Photo courtesy of Angelo Barovier/Barovier & Toso*

Bimini Werkstätte

In 1923 Fritz Lampl (1892-1955) founded a studio in Vienna with architects and brothers Artur (1891-1981) and Josef Berger (1898-1989). Lampl named it Bimini and almost immediately won international acclaim for high artistic standards. The product was practically weightless and delicate —either thinly blown drinking glasses or whimsical lampwork animals and figures. The only markings were paper labels, which have rarely survived, but the distinctive Art Deco style can be easily recognized. Diagonal filigree, although in the Venetian style, can be distinguished from fifties Murano glass, by its featherweight construction. The workshop closed in 1938. (Neuwirth 1992 461-463)

Blenko

After several false starts (beginning in 1893) by English born William John Blenko, the company began in 1915 in Milton, West Virginia. In 1923 Blenko's son William H. (Bill) joined and then continued to run Blenko Glass after his father's death in 1933. William Anderson, the first full-time designer, was hired in 1946. From then on, they became a leading American producer of mold-blown and free blown tableware in rich vibrant colors, sometimes combined with clear glass. Typical fifties features include thick walls with controlled air bubbles and asymmetrical forms such as pinched and folded vases similar to the fazzoletto.

Boda

Founded in 1864 in southern Sweden, it merged with Kosta in 1946.

Cenedese & C.

The company was established in 1946 in Murano by Gino Cenedese, who also served as art director. Alfredo Barbini became a partner in 1947 and left in 1950. Fulvio Bianconi designed for Cenedese in the mid-50s. Pieces are often not signed or labeled, but both paper labels and engraved signatures can be found.

Daum & Cie

Jean Daum began a glass workshop in Nancy, France in 1875 which has stayed continuously in the family. The company was very important for colorful Art Nouveau and Art Deco glass. Henri and Michel Daum concentrated on clear crystal in the 1950s.

Erickson Glassworks

A defunct glass factory in Bremen, Ohio was purchased by Swedish-born brothers Carl and Steven Erickson in 1943. Carl designed most of the mold-blown glass, distinguished by heavy casing, controlled bubbles, and frequently, a heavy ball of glass for a base. They were identified by a yellow and blue paper label, and free-formed pieces had an engraved signature. The company closed in 1961. (Knower 2-5)

Flygsfors

Flygsfors was founded in 1888 in Sweden, was purchased by Orrefors in the 1970s, but closed by 1980. In 1949 Paul Kedelv joined the company, and throughout the 50s designed the "Coquille" series of sculptural vessels in biomorphic shapes with thick transparent casing over opaque shapes. The pieces have an engraved signature, but can be easily identified without. Other companies, including Erickson in the United States, imitated the style of some bowls.

Fratelli Toso

The company was founded in 1854 in Murano by the five Toso brothers. Ermanno Toso was artistic director from the 1930s and worked with his sons Giusto and Renato, who later took over. Their postwar work is distinguished by colorful fused murrhine or canes and is rarely signed, but paper labels are sometimes found.

Hadeland

Founded in 1762 in Norway, Hadeland made colorful glass bottles from 1765. The company was sold in 1824. The first full-time designer joined in 1929, followed by successes at Milan Triennales in the 1930s. Art glass production increased when Herman Bongard and Willy Johansson began designing in 1947. Recently, Hadeland has produced 80 per cent of Norway's glass. (Opie 175, Polak 72)

Holmegaard

Founded in 1825 in Denmark, the company made dark green bottles followed by service glass production beginning in 1835. Glass-blowers were brought from Bohemia and southern Germany for hand-formed glass production. The first full-time designer joined in 1923, followed by Jacob Bang in 1925, and by Per Lütken in 1941. It merged with Kastrup in 1965 and then with Royal Copenhagen in 1975. (Grover 95, Opie 175)

Iittala

Founded in 1881 in Finland, in 1915 it merged with (or was sold to) Ahlstrom, which had already acquired Karhula in 1917. Tapio Wirkkala became chief designer in 1946 and designed the famous "Kantterelli" vase in that year. Timo Sarpeneva joined in 1950, the year that Kaj Franck left. Iittala produced fifty percent of Finland's glass in the 1950s and merged with Nuutajärvi in 1987. (Beard 210, Eidelberg 377, Opie 176)

Vetro,
legno e argento
di Tapio Wirkkala

Tapio Wirkkala continua la sua
produzione in questi tre settori:
compensati scavati, in forme di
vasi e di decorazioni, vetri per
Karhula Iittala, argenti per la
Kultakeskus (abbiamo da poco
pubblicato le sue nuove posate,
la cui produzione interessa an-
che la Rosenthal). Ha avuto inol-
tre l'incarico dal governo finlan-
dese di disegnare delle nuove ban-
conote (potrebbe capitare una co-
sa simile in Italia?). In questi
mesi Tapio Wirkkala è in America; a Washington, presso la
Smithsonian Institution ci sarà
una mostra di pezzi suoi e di ce-
ramiche della moglie Rut Bryk.

Vasi per Karhula Iittala

Karhula Iittala vases designed by Tapio Wirkkala *Photo courtesy of ©Domus (319:54, June 1956)*

Kastrup

Founded in 1845 in Denmark, by the same family that founded Holmegaard, Kastrup became the first Danish producer of pressed glass in the 1880s. Kastrup merged with Holmegaard in 1965. (Grover 96)

Kosta, Kosta Boda

The earliest glass factory still working in Sweden, Kosta was founded in 1742, became a public stock company in 1875, and attracted attention with Gallé imitations at the end of the 19th century. Encouraged by the Swedish Society of Industrial Design, they began hiring artists as designers in 1917. The company went through many name changes and mergers. Åfors gained control before WWII, and Kosta merged with Åfors and Boda in 1946. Vicke Lindstrand became art director in 1950 and brought techniques previously used at Orrefors, such as Ariel and Graal. Kosta was a very significant art glass producer in the 1950s and remains a leading producer of high quality art glass. (Eidelberg 380, Opie 176)

Leerdam (Koninklijke Nederlandsche Glasfabriek Leerdam)

Leerdam was founded in 1765 at Leerdam, the Netherlands and made ordinary tableware and utilitarian glass. Its modern work began when P.M. Cochius, who was influenced by the De Stijl style, became director in 1912. Andries Copier became associated in 1914 at the age of 13, became artistic supervisor in 1923, and artistic director in 1927. Floris Meydam joined in 1935 and created the Unica line. (Beard 211, Eidelberg 380)

Nuutajärvi-Notsjö

The oldest surviving glassworks in Finland, the company was established in 1793 and made window and bottle glass. In the mid-19th century it produced filigree and pressed glass, but its significant artistic contribution began when Gunnel Nyman (1909-1948) was artistic director from 1946-1948. Kaj Franck was a designer and then artistic director from 1950-1976 (while also working at Arabia from 1945-1960). Oiva Toikka became artistic director in 1963, and the company merged with Iittala in 1988 to form Iittala-Nuutajärvi. (Beard 212, Eidelberg 389, Opie 177)

Orrefors

An ironworks was founded at Orrefors, Sweden in 1726. They began making glass bottles in 1898, and cameo glass was produced briefly in 1913. Then the painters, Simon Gate and Edward Hald, were hired as designers in 1916 and 1917 respectively. They developed the Graal technique, which was based on the cameo process but then encased in thick clear glass. The Ariel technique, an extension of Graal but with trapped air bubbles, was developed in 1937 by Vicke Lindstrand, Edvin Ohrström, and Gustav Bergkvist. Orrefors was the major Swedish company to dominate art glass in the 1950s. It includes a glass-making school and the Orrefors Museum, which opened in 1957. (Eidelberg 390, Opie 177, Orrefors Gallery 84/85)

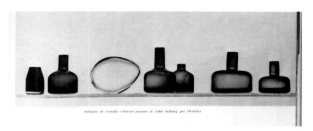

bottiglie in cristallo colorato presente di John Selbing per Orrefors

Orrefors exhibit *Photo courtesy of ©Domus (336:5, Nov. 1957)*

Pukeberg

Founded in 1871 in Sweden, it was bought by a lamp manufacturer and began producing lamps in 1894. The production of decorative glasswares began in the 1930s and became more important in 1959 when designers such as Ann and Göran Wärff joined the firm. (Opie 178)

Riihimäki

Founded in 1910 in Finland by M. A. Kolehmainen (former technical director at Karhula) and his son, Riihimäki produced blown glass from 1919 to 1924. The company sponsored design competitions in 1928 and in the 1930s. It gained international recognition after the war. Riihimäki ceased blown glass production in 1976 and was taken over by Ahlstrom in 1985. (Beard 210-11, Opie 178)

Salviati & Co.

Founded in the 1850s by Antonio Salviati in Murano, the company was active in the revival of Venetian glass in the 19th century. In 1896 Maurice Camerino managed the glassworks, then became sole proprietor. His sons, Mario and Renzo, became active in the 1920s, and designers such as Luciano Gaspari worked for them. Gaspari was followed by Dino Martens, who designed in the 1930s. Salviati won several international awards, including the Compasso d'Oro, for its long tradition of excellence. The company was sold in 1987. (Beard 213, Fifty-50, Grover 139)

Vetraria Archimede Seguso

The company was created in 1946 by Archimede Seguso, who had left Seguso Vetri d'Arte in 1942. He was his own chief designer and artistic director and is especially noted for the "merletto" technique using a variety of fine lacework and netted patterns, in addition to the use of color gradations and sprays of metallic flecks. His combination of orignial designs and fine craftsmanship have made Archimede Seguso one of the important masters of Murano. (Heiremans cat nos 97-112)

Seguso Vetri d'Arte

The company was created in 1932 by Archimede Seguso, Napoleane Barovier, Antonio Ernesto, Olimpo Ferro, and the brothers Angelo and Bruno Seguso. It was called Artistica Vetreria e Soffiera Barovier Seguso e Ferro for one year, until Ferro left and it became Seguso Vetri d'Arte. They collaborated with Vittorio Zecchin in the beginning and exhibited at Venice Biennales in 1934 and 1938. Archimede Seguso became the maestro di prima piazza, while Flavio Poli was artistic director from 1937-1963. Poli is known for his use of the "sommerso" technique, in which thick layers of colored glass appear to float inside other layers. Archimede Seguso left in 1942 to form his own glassworks. Of the many postwar successes, the "valva" series won the Compasso d'Oro in 1954. Although etched signatures were used in the 1930s and 40s, and some pieces are engraved "Seguso," most are unsigned. (Deboni & Cocchi 120, Franzoi 18 & 32, Heiremans cat nos 113-128)

Skruf

Established in 1897 in Sweden, Skruf made simple household wares, went bankrupt in 1908, and reorganized in 1909. The factory burned down in 1946 and was rebuilt. The first full-time staff designer, Bengt Edenfalk, joined in 1953 and participated in major international exhibitions, including Milan Triennales. They were purchased by Boda in 1977. (Opie 179)

Steuben

Frederick Carder (1863-1963) established a glass factory at Corning, New York in 1903. A genius for both design and execution of techniques, Carder is known for his work in the Art Nouveau and Art Deco styles. The factory developed into the Steuben Glass Co. (in Steuben County) in 1933 as a division of the Corning Glass Company and ceased production of colored glass. A formal design department was established in 1936, and the Corning Glass Center was built in 1951 to house the Corning Museum of Glass with its research library and the Steuben factory for the production of the finest crystal. (Beard 213, Madigan)

Strömbergshyttan

Founded in 1876 in Sweden as the Lindfors Glasbruk, the company was purchased by former Orrefors head, Edward Strömberg in 1943. Gerda Strömberg (1879-1960) designed glass from 1933-55. It was sold to Orrefors in 1975 and closed in 1979. (Opie 179)

Venini & C.

The company was founded in 1921 in Murano by Paolo Venini, a lawyer from a glassmaking family, Andrea Rioda, a Venetian glass factory owner, and Giacomo Cappellin, an antique Venetian glass dealer. It was incorporated in 1924 as Vetri Soffiati Muranesi Venini Cappellin & C., and hired the most creative and talented artists and designers, including the Muranese painter, Vittorio Zecchin, as art director. In 1925 Cappellin withdrew to form his own glass company, and Francesco Zecchin and sculptor Napoleone Martinuzzi joined Venini. Martinuzzi became art director but left with Zecchin in 1932, so Carlo Scarpa, who left Maestri Vetrai Muranesi Cappellin, was hired as a designer in the same year. In 1938 Scarpa exhibited heavy sculptural pieces in Sweden. This began the collaboration between Venini and Scandinavian companies through exhibits and the hiring of designers, such as Tapio Wirkkala. Fulvio Bianconi arrived in 1948. The company is noted for the revival of filigree techniques and innovative use of canes and murrhine. It is considered to be the most important of all 20th century Murano glassworks, especially during Venini's lifetime. When Venini died in 1959, Ludovico Diaz de Santillana took over the company. Through the years, some of the important collaborators have included Eugenè Berman, Fulvio Bianconi, Riccardo Licata, Tobia Scarpa, Thomas Stearns, Lyn Tissot, Massimo Vignelli, Tapio Wirkkala, and Toni Zuccheri. (Deboni 14-28, Deboni & Cocchi 122, Eidelberg 403, Smithsonian 12-15)

Venini in Europe *Photo courtesy of © Domus (361:43, Dec. 1959)*

Venini glass *Photo courtesy © Domus (314:45, Jan. 1956)*

Venini glass *Photo courtesy of © Domus (361:40/41 insert, Dec. 1959)*

Venini advertisement *Photo courtesy of © Domus (323:56, Oct. 1956)*

Vetreria Vistosi

Founded in 1945 by Gugliemo Vistosi, Vetreria Vistosi's most creative work was done in the 1960s, usually form-blown with enclosed decoration of glass pieces and murrina. Designers include the names Luciano and Gino Vistosi, Fulvio Bianconi, and Austrian, Ettore Sottsass. Paper labels were used. (Heiremans cat nos 224-238)5.1 BT-01

163

CHAPTER VI

Labels and Signatures

Signatures and labels are valuable for the collector and researcher because they not only identify one piece, they lead to attribution of others by comparison. Not all fifties glass is signed or labeled, and many pieces once had paper labels that have since been lost. Scandinavian glass of the period usually has an engraved marking at the base. This can range from a complete designer signature with company name, design name, and a number code which can date the piece, to an abbreviated mark of only initials and/or numbers. For example, Orrefors used the complete form for marking special designer series, such as Edward Hald's "Fishgraal" vase, while Kosta used the initials LH on hand-formed pieces designed by Vicke Lindstrand. The signature does not make the work valuable, but the information it holds can enhance an already meritorious piece.

Italian glass, however, is frequently found without an identifying mark. An exception would be Venini, which has usually taken care to identify the company's work with an acid stamp on the base. This mark is sometimes difficult to find and to read. The piece must be tilted and moved slowly until the light catches this stamped signature at just the right angle. Venini also used paper labels, with or without the acid stamp, and, not surprisingly, these labels are often missing. But since so many Venini pieces were signed, identification by comparison, especially if one is familiar with the high quality of glass they produced, is often possible. A.V.E.M. did not sign their work. Seguso, Barovier & Toso, and others frequently used only paper labels. Some companies are not identified by name and only used one of many generic "Venetian Glass" or "Murano Glass" paper stickers. This makes the field somewhat confusing, but it also creates an intriguing situation for collectors and researchers, where a keen eye and a good memory can substitute for a deep pocket. Unlike well-established fields, with little remaining likelihood of finding the sleepers that tintillate collectors' imaginations, fifties glass presents undiscovered opportunities and enjoyment. Except for the consistent and methodical code engraved on Swedish glass, the following sample of signatures and labels may be more of a curiosity than a real aid to research. What are now required are more "Rosetta stones," identified or well-attributed examples of glass, which will enable classification of unmarked pieces by comparing quality, design, technique, and the magic emitted when the light strikes them.

Information on Orrefors signatures and numbering systems was provided by Orrefors.

Orrefors Designer Signatures
A Olle Alberius
B Gunnar Cyrén
D Ingeborg Lundin
F Edvin Ohrström
G Simon Gate
H Edward Hald
J Jan Johansson
K Henning Koppel
L Vicke Lindstrand
N Nils Landberg
P Sven Palmqvist
R Carl Fagerlund
S John Selbing
T Lars Hellsten
V Eva Englund

After 1980, two initials were used for these designer signatures, ie. EH Edward Hald. Orrefor's marks designating the type of glass are placed after the designer initial. For example, A for cut glass after H for Hald, HA cut glass by Edward Hald. This should not be confusing as long as the type of glass is apparent. Since, for example, frosted glass is easily recognized, the HE need not be confused with EH, or Hald unfrosted glass.
A cut glass
E frosted (satin ground)
U workshop made, smooth glass
Z green lustrous glass
Graal-S or S-Graal for slipgraal

Numbering Ariel
1950 51 B-52 B; 53 E-832 E
1951 833 E-1450 E
1952 1451 E-1755 E
1953 1756 E-2022 E
1954 2023 E-2203 E
1955 50 F-242 F
1956 243 F-408 F 1957 409 F-572 F
1958 100 G-226 G
1959 100 H-267 H
1960 268 H-711 H

Numbering Slip-graal
1950 51 B-52 B; 53 L-399 L
1951 400 L-847 L
1952 848 L-1175 L
1953 1176 L-1600 L
1954 1601 L-2308 L
1955 2309 L-23 10 L; 50 M-433 M
1956 100 N-289 N
1957 51 0-225 0
1958 226 0-344 0
1959 345 P-440 P
1960 441 P-558 P

Numbering Ravenna
1948 1-8
1949 9-10
1950 1 1-18 1951 1 9-22
1952 287-365
1953 366-608
1954 609-743
1955 744-9 13
1956 914-1078
1957 1079-1219
1958 1220-1343
1959 1344-1567
1960 1568-1725

Numbering Fishgraal
1945 2261-2355
1946 2356-2824
1947 2825-2999; 300 B-650 B
1948 651 B-1660 B
1949 1661 B-1999 B; 200 C-869 C
1950 870 C-1914 C
1951 1915 C-2999 C; 200 D-437 D
1952 438 D-1835 D
1953 1836 D-2866 D
1954 2867 D-3000 D; 200 H-1386 H
1955 1387 K-2547 K
1956 101 L-1276 L
1957 101 M-1294 IVI
1958 100 N-1204 N
1959 100 Q-1134 Q
1960 100 P-963 P

Kosta
Kosta pieces designed by Vicke Lindstrand are
sometimes signed with the full name. An initial code
beginning with an L for Lindstrand is often used.
LH hand-shaped by Lindstrand. 1955/56 catalog
nos. 1001-1259; 1958 catalog nos. 1265-1627; 1962/63
catalog nos. 1640-1784
LU Unica. 1955/56 nos. 2004-2036
LC hand-shaped colora. 1955/56 nos. 1-11
LF hand-shaped birds. 1955/56 nos. 1-7
LG engraved. 1955/56 nos.101-212; 1959 nos. 213-
330; 1962 nos. 335-407
LS cut. 1955/56 nos. 501-590; 1959 nos. 213-330; 1962
nos. 683-754 (Ricke & Gronert, 290)
Italian glass is more difficult to date. Styles of
signatures and paper labels can indicate approximate
years of production. For example, Venini used
several acid stamped marks:

The following illustrations are a sample of the kinds
of identifying marks used on fifties glass:

Alfredo Barbini Venetian Made by Alfredo
Barbini for Weil Ceramics & Glass Murano Italy

Barovier & Toso Barovier & Toso Murano Made in Italy

Cenedese Murano Cenedese Vetri

Cenedese Cenedese Glass Murano 28/75 Made in Italy

Cenedese

Salviati Made in Italy Salviati E. Murano

Salviati Salviati & Co. Venice Made in Italy

Salviati

Archimede Seguso Archimede Seguso Murano Made in Italy

Archimede Seguso Made in Murano Italy

Seguso Vetri d'Arte Seguso Vetri d'Arte Murano Made in Italy

Venini Venini S. A. Murano (with vase)

Fratelli Toso Murano Glass Made in Italy

Murano Glass Murano Glass Made in Italy

Made in Italy

Murano Murano Made in Italy (with rooster)

Vetro Artistico Veneziano Hand Made Genuine Venetian
Glass Vetro Artistico Veneziano Made in Murano Italy

Genuine Venetian Glass Genuine Venitian Glass Made in
Italy

Kastrup Holmegaard Kastrup Holmegaard Made in Denmark by appointment to H. M. the King (with swan and crown)

Higgins

Kosta Kosta Sweden (foil crown, circa 1950s)

Kosta Kosta Sweden (crown)

Kosta Boda Kosta Boda Sweden Limited Edition by
Bertil Vallien (1970s)

Kosta Boda Kosta Boda AB Sweden Handmade
(1980s)

Nuutajärvi-Notsjö Nuutajärvi-Notsjö 1793 Suomi
Finland

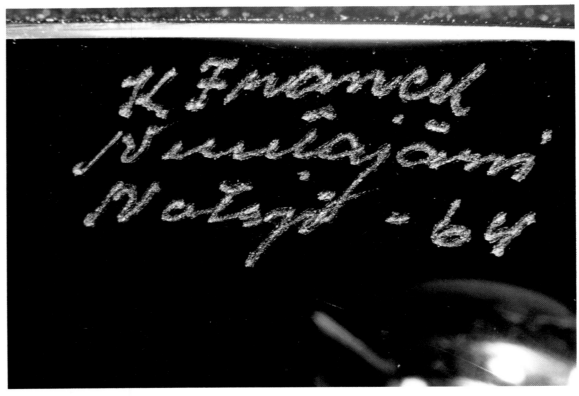

Kaj Franck K. Franck Nuutajärvi-Notsjö 64

Edward Hald Orrefors Graal Nr. 234 S Edward Hald
(1962)

Edward Hald Orrefors Graal
Nr. 236 E 3 Edward Hald
(1973)

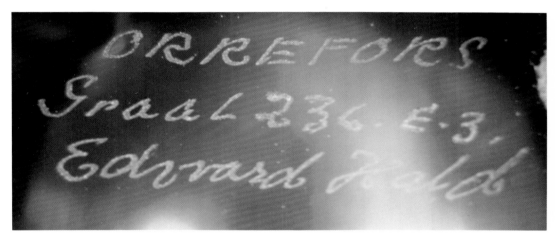

Tapio Wirkkala

Pukeberg Pukeberg Sweden

Riihimäki Kumela Riihimäki Made in Finland
(glass-blower)

Skruf Skruf Sweden (crown and cross)

Snowflakes Made in China

CHAPTER VII

Glossary

Ariel
The technique developed by Edvin Ohrström, Vicke Lindstrand, and Gustav Bergkvist at Orrefors in 1937, is similar to Graal, but controlled air bubbles trapped in cut-out patterns in the glass are used to make the design. The name is after the spirit in Shakespeare's *Tempest*.

Aventurina, aventurine
In the 15th century aventurine glass achieved its metallic effect by using gold inclusions; since the 17th century the same effect has been accomplished by combining copper particles with the hot glass.

Bullicante
Air bubbles are placed in a regular pattern in the glass.

Calcedonio, chalcedony
This opaque glass resembles chalcedony, the semi-precious stone and type of agate.

Cane
Canes are glass rods used in striped glass and twisted filigree or sliced so that sections of polychrome patterns can be used in mosaic or murrhine glass.

Cased
Two or more layers of different colored glass are blown, one over the other.

Cristallo
Italian soda glass (the barilla plant is burned to make soda ash) is easily worked, clear and transparent, and similar in appearance to rock crystal. It was perfected by Angelo Barovier in the mid-15th century and called cristallo.

Fazzoletto
The fazzoletto or handkerchief-shaped vase was originally designed by Fulvio Bianconi for Venini in 1949 and became one of the most famous fifties shapes.

Filigrana, filigree
Filigrana is a technique using glass threads or fine canes twisted around a clear cane or embedded in clear glass to produce either fine net-like patterns or parallel threading. Similar terms include latticino and zanfirico.

Gold leaf, silver leaf
Pieces of gold or silver leaf applied to the hot glass break up into flakes of various sizes and minute particles as the vessel is blown.

Graal
This technique was developed at Orrefors by designers Simon Gate and Edward Hald with glassblower Knut Bergkvist. The pattern is cut into a core of colored glass, (similar to cameo glass, but actually in reverse, since the cut-away part forms the design rather than the background), then encased in clear glass and blown into its final shape.

Incalmo
Two gathers of hot glass are fused, permitting the combination of distinct colors or techniques on a single vessel.

Kraka
This decorative technique, developed by Sven Palmqvist at Orrefors, resembles an intricate fishnet encased in glass, similar to the Muranese reticello.

Lampwork
Lampwork refers to forming delicate objects out of thin rods or canes while working at the "lamp," or a small flame.

Latticino
Filigree in stripes or net-like patterns, originally of white glass threads, and later to include colors, is among the most distinctive techniques used in Murano.

Lattimo

This opaque white glass, or milk glass (latte=milk), resembles porcelain when used to case or form a vessel; it is also used in various filigree techniques.

Merletto

There are two versions of this lacework design: one, developed by Archimede Seguso in 1952, is a type of latticino using fine threads of glass; the other, by Venini, produces a similar effect by using an acid etching technique.

Mezza filigrana

The term mezza filigrana, or half filigree, is used for filigree threads running diagonally and parallel to each other, as well as for wider rods creating a diagonal striped pattern.

Millefiori

In this type of murrhine glass, slices of multicolored canes are embedded in clear glass to create a "thousand flower" design.

Mosaica, mosaic

Pieces of colored glass, such as murrine, are fused into the vessel.

Murrina, murrhine

In this mosaic technique, colored cane sections are embedded into the hot glass before the piece is blown into its final shape. In ancient Rome "murra" referred to an ornamental precious stone used in making vases and other articles, and "murrini" was the ancient mosaic glass technique. The terms "murrina" and "murrine." (English "murrhine") were adjectives meaning "made of murra," but in the late nineteenth century were used to describe the ancient mosaic glass. More recently, these terms have also come to be used to describe the mosaic pieces or slices of canes used in the technique.

Pezzato

Literally meaning patchwork, Barovier and Toso are especially noted for this technique.

Pulegoso

Literally bubbled (a puliga is an air bubble), the technique uses randomly placed air bubbles of various sizes which sometimes burst on the surface of the glass like little craters.

Ariel

Ravenna
Developed by Sven Palmqvist at Orrefors, a layer of colored glass is decorated with a pattern of inlaid colored glass (usually mosaic-like), then covered with another layer of glass and blown into its final shape.

Reticello (filigrana a reticello)
In this netted filigree, the threads criss-cross diagonally, usually with an air bubble in each diamond shape enclosed by the threads.

Retortoli (filigrana a retortoli)
This twisted filigree in a spiral shape is also called zanfirico.

Rod
A rod is a monochrome cane, but the term cane is usually used.

Sfumato
This technique produces a smoky effect by enclosing fine inner veils of color in the glass.

Sommerso
Small particles or larger colored glass shapes are encased in clear or differently colored thick glass, usually producing a heavy and sculptural effect.

Tessuto
Literally meaning fabric, spiral filigree or groups of canes produce a fabric or lace effect.

Zanfirico
Twenty distinct styles of the zanfirico technique used by Venini are illustrated in Deboni, p. 219. Other terms include filigrano, latticino, and a retortoli.

Aventurine

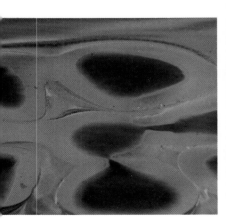

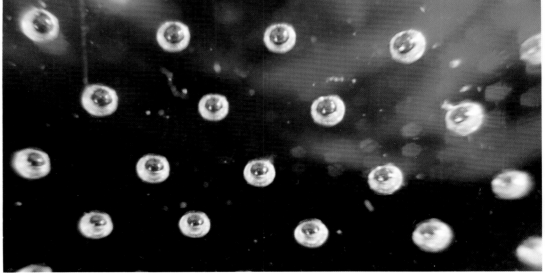

Bullicante

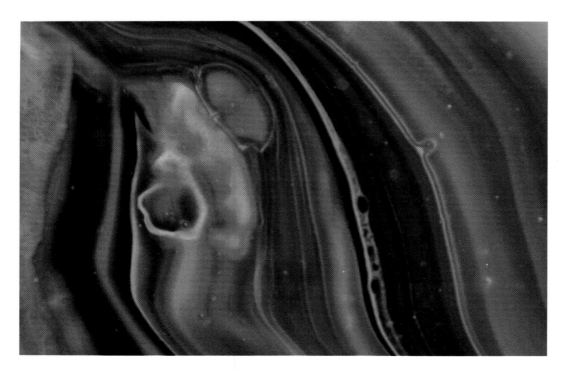

Calcedonio or Chalcedony

Canes

Cane pieces

Cased

Fazzoletto

Filigrana

Gold leaf

Gold leaf

Silver leaf

Graal

Incalmo

Opposite page:
Gold and silver leaf

Kraka *Photo courtesy of Orrefors*

Latticino

Latticino

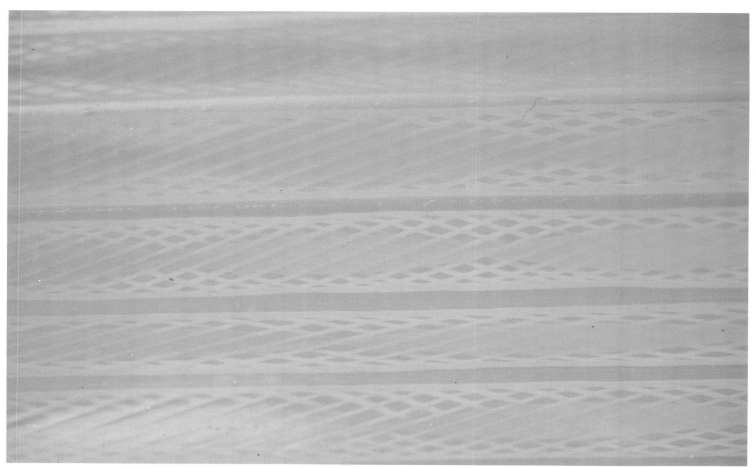

Latticino

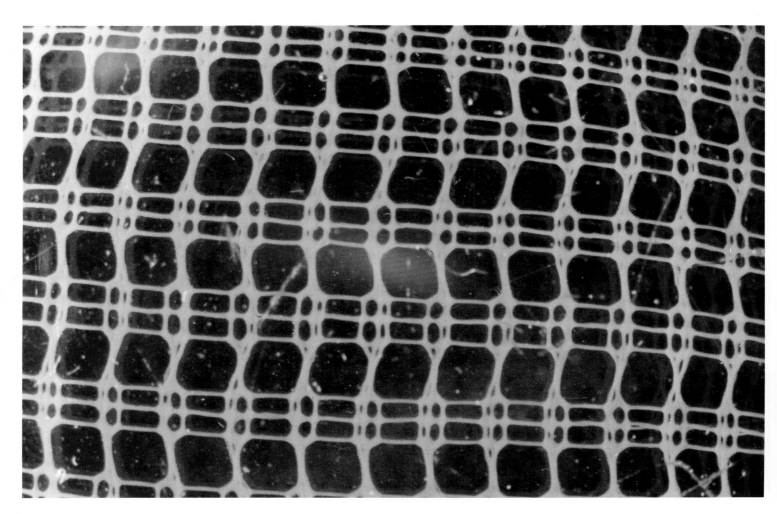

Merletto

Mezza filigrana

Mezza filigrana

Mezza filigrana

Millefiori

Mosaica

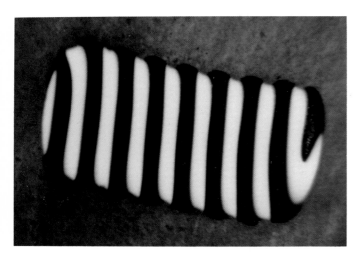

Murrine

Murrine

Murrine *Photo courtesy of Sotheby's*

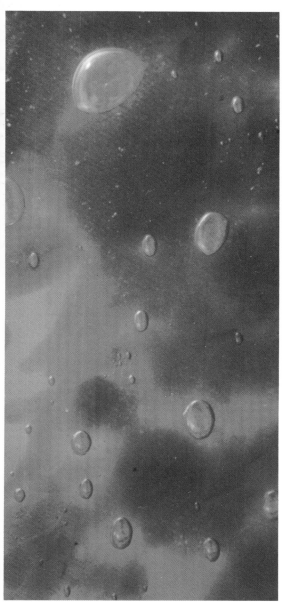

Pulegoso

Pezzato *Photo courtesy of Sotheby's*

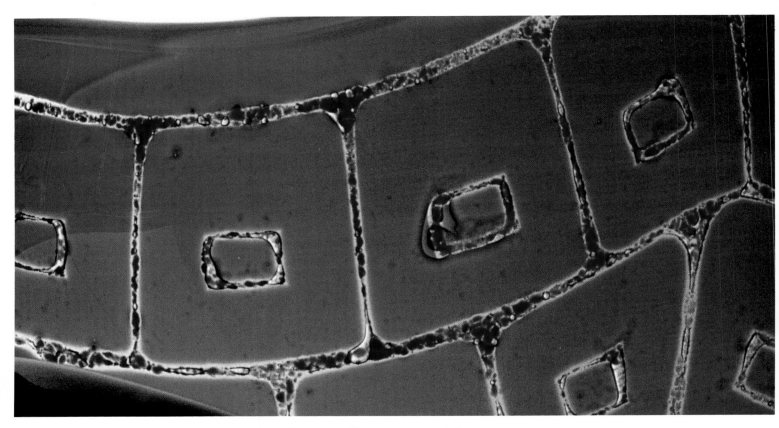

Ravenna *Photo courtesy of Orrefors*

Reticello

Retortoli

Retortoli

Sfumato

Sommerso

Sommerso

Tessuto *Photo courtesy of Sotheby's*

Zanfirico

Zanfirico

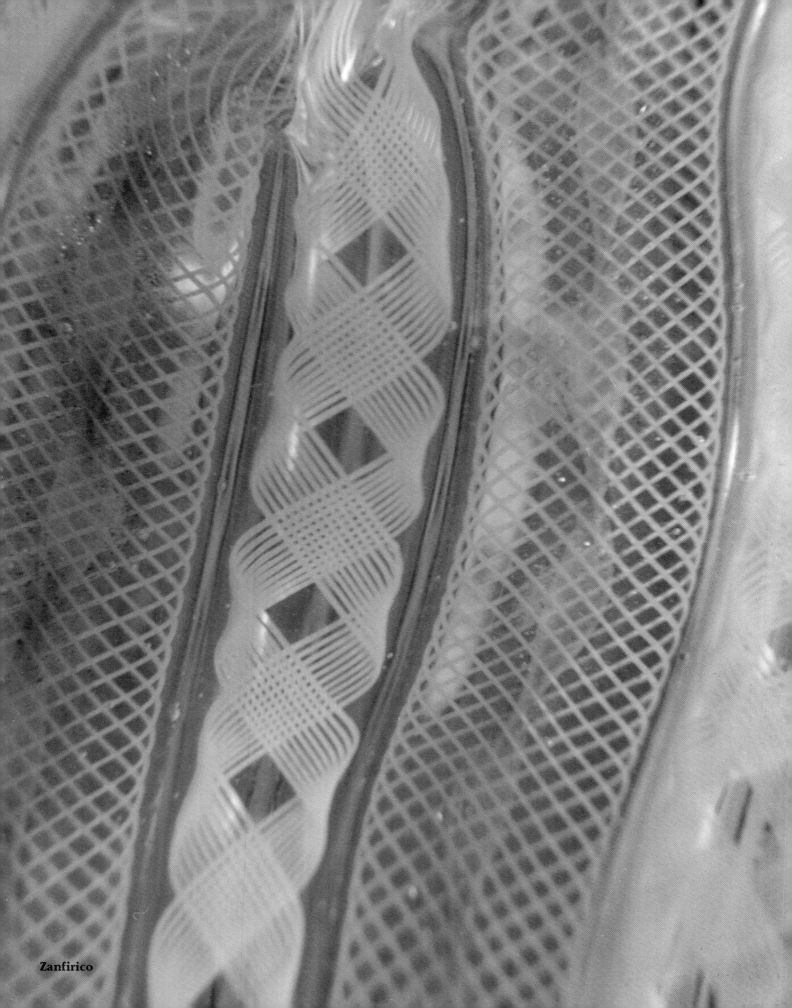

Zanfirico

Select Bibliography

Aloi, Roberto. *Esempi Vetri D'oggi di Decorazione Moderna di Tutto il Mondo.* Milan: Ulrico Hoepli, 1955. Black and white illustrations make this a useful reference. (Italian text)

Beard, Geoffrey. *International Modern Glass.* New York: Charles Scribner's Sons, 1976. A lengthy section on glass manufacturers and artists is included.

Cappa, Giuseppe. *L'Europe de L'Art Verrier 1850-1990.* Liège, Belgium: Pierre Mardaga, 1991. A good section on fifties glass is included. (French text)

Christie's *Arts Décoratifs D xxeme Siecle.* Monaco, Feb. 1, 1987.

Modern Illustrated Books and Twentieth Century Decorative Arts. Geneva, Nov. 8, 1987.

Robots, Spacetoys, and Post-War Glass. Amsterdam, May 2, 1988.

Property from the Estate of Robert Mapplethorpe. New York, Oct. 31, 1989.

These auction catalogs are especially good for fifties glass, while other catalogs from the Twentieth Century Decorative Arts category also include examples. Current auction catalogs are among the best sources for understanding market trends and prices, while past catalogs are excellent references for identification and study. Christie's and Sotheby's set the standards and reflect the international markets.

Corning Museum of Glass. *Glass 1959.* Corning, New York: Corning Museum, 1959. This contemporary catalog of an international exhibit of modern glass with black and white illustrations is a classic.

New Glass Review. Corning, New York, 1982-present. The latest examples of glass art plus an extensive bibliography of recent publications about glass are featured in this illustrated annual.

Deboni, Franco. *I Vetri Venini.* Torino: Umberto Allemandi & Co., 1989. This lavishly illustrated monograph includes detailed technical information, artist biographies, and history of Venini. (Italian text)

Deboni, Franco & Maurizio Cocchi. *Vetri di Murano del '900: 50 Capolavori.* Milan: In Arte, 1991. This beautifully illustrated exhibition catalog includes works by the major companies in Murano with a section on company histories and artist biographies. (Italian text)

Decorative Art Studio Yearbook. London: The Studio Limited. This annual publication is an excellent contemporary source for articles and illustrations of objects, in this case, from the fifties.

Domus. Milan: Editoriale Domus, 1928-present. Some of the best contemporary photographs of high style interior design and decorative arts can be found in this Italian periodical.

Don Treadway Gallery. *Important Italian Glass.* Cincinnati: Don Treadway and Ripleys' Antiques Galleries, November 15, 1992. This auction catalog of 256 lots of Italian glass, with a focus on the 1950s, is an excellent source for identification and pricing. It also includes two pages of illustrated labels.

Dorigato, Attilia. *Ercole Barovier 1889-1974: Vetraio Muranese.* Venice: Marsilio Editori, 1989. The color illustrations and chronology of Barovier's work make this one of the best references on the subject. (Italian text)

Murano il Vetro a Tavola Ieri e Oggi. Venice: Museo Vetrario, 1983. Good illustrations make this a useful reference. (Italian text)

Eidelberg, Martin, ed. *Design 1935-1965.* New York: Abrams, 1991. Le Musée desArts Décoratifs de Montréal put together an outstanding traveling exhibiton of decorative arts representing the period. This monumental catalog contains a wealth of information on artists, designers, companies, and design history.

Eige, Eason & Rick Wilson. *Blenko Glass 1930-1953*. Marietta, Ohio: Antique Publications, 1987. In addition to good color illustrations of the glass, the book includes a company history with early photographs and reprints from company catalogs.

Fifty-50. *Venini & the Murano Renaissance: Italian Art Glass of the 1940s & 50s*. New York: Fifty-50, 1984. This small but beautifully illustrated exhibition catalog also includes information on companies.

Finnish Society of Crafts and Design. *Tapio Wirkkala*. Helsinki: Finnish Society of Crafts and Design, 1985. Biographical information, philosophy, and lovely illustrations present the artist and his work.

Franzoi, Umberto, ed. *Art Glass by Archimede Seguso*. Venice: Arsenale Editrice, 1991. This beautiful catalog is among the best sources for examples of Seguso's glass and information about the artist and company.

Grover, Ray & Lee. *Contemporary Art Glass*. New York: Crown, 1975. The work of 96 glass artists is presented, including information on some fifties artists and companies.

Habsburg, Feldman. *Twentieth Century Decorative Arts*. Geneva: May 13 & 14, 1990. This well-illustrated auction catalog has an excellent section on fifties glass.

Heirmans, Marc. *Murano Glas 1945-1970*. Antwerp: Gallery Novecento, 1989. The text is brief, but the contemporary and new photographs make this small soft cover book an excellent reference for identifying Murano glass of the period. (German and English text)

Glas-Kunst-Glaser 1910-1970 Italienische This book was scheduled for Spring 1993 and not yet available as this book was going to press.

Herlitz-Gezelius, Ann Marie. *Kosta: The Glass and the Artists*. Sweden: Bokforlaget Signum, 1987. Illustrations and a short section on labels and signatures are useful. (Swedish text)

Jackson, Lesley. *The New Look: Design in the Fifties*. New York: Thames and Hudson, 1991. This well-illustrated catalog of an exhibition by the Manchester City Art Galleries has examples of glass scattered throughout plus a short section on fifties glass.

Katonah Gallery. *Art by Design: Reflections of Finland*. Katonah, New York: Katonah Gallery, 1989. This small but very nice catalog of works includes artist biographies.

Klein, Dan & Margaret Bishop. *Decorative Art 1880-1980*. Oxford: Phaidon, and Christie's, 1986. This survey, including a chapter on postwar design, is illustrated with objects from Christie's auctions with prices.

Klein, Dan & Ward Lloyd, eds. *The History of Glass*. London: Orbis, 1984. There are many good general surveys about glass, but this one has an especially nice chapter on glass since 1945.

Knower, Ramona & Franklin. *Erickson Freehand Glass*. Columbus, Ohio: Knower, 1971. Color and black-and-white photographs make this little catalog useful for identifying the glass.

Liège, Musée Curtius. *Aspects de la verrerie contemporaine*. Liège, Belgium, Musée Curtius, 1958. Black and white illustrations make this contemporay exhibition catalog a useful reference. (French text)

Madigan, Mary Jean. *Steuben Glass: An American Tradition in Crystal*. New York: Harry N. Abrams, 1982. A beautifully illustrated history of the company and catalog with photographs, line drawings, and artist biographies. This book is an excellent reference and resource for collectors.

Mariacher, Giovanni. *I Vetri Di Murano*. Milan: Carlo Bestetti, 1967. This multi-lingual history of Venetian glass includes good color illustrations of glass by the major companies.

McFadden, David Revere, ed. *Scandinavian Modern Design 1880-1980*. New York: Abrams, 1982. This nicely illustrated and useful source includes biographical information on many of the artists known for fifties glass.

Mentasti, Rosa Barovier. *Glass in Murano*. Venice: Chamber of Commerce, 1984. Examples of work from glass making companies currently operating in Murano are nicely presented together with essays on history and technology.

Vetro Veneziano 1890-1990 Venice: Arsenale Editrice; 1992. This is one of the best books on Venetian glass written in English and includes a chapter on the 50s. The color illustrations are dramatic and wonderful.

Mille Anni di Arte del Vetro o Venezia. Venice: Albrizzi, 1982. This excellent illustrated reference on Venetian glass from the earliest examples up to the present was reprinted in 1988. (Italian text)

Neuwirth, Waltraud. *Italian Glass 1950-1960.* Vienna: Waltraud Neuwirth, 1987. This exhibition catalog in English, French, German, and Italian is one of the best sources for identifying pieces from contemporary black and white and recent color illustrations.

Bimini: Wiener Glaskunst des Art Deco. Vienna: Waltraud Neuwirth, 1992. This illustrated book on a very distinctive style of glass should enable identification and help to eliminate any confusion between Bimini and Murano glass from the 50s. (German text with English summary)

Ohira, Yoichi. *A Guide to Venetian Glass.* Padora: Edizioni, 1991. This brief, but nicely illustrated glossary of 16 terms is in Italian, English, German, French, Spanish, and Japanese.

Opie, Jennifer Hawkins. *Scandinavian Ceramics and Glass in the Twentieth Century.* New York: Rizzoli, 1990. Historical background, excellent artist biographies and company histories, are included in this well illustrated exhibition catalog.

Orrefors Gallery 1984-85. Orrefors, Sweden, 1985. Produced by Orrefors, this beautiful little book includes artist biographies, a short company history, and illustrations of fifties and other glass. Later Gallery books such as 1990 and 1992 feature outstanding recent examples.

Polak, Ada. *Modern Glass.* New York: Thomas Yoseloff, 1962. Good black and white illustrations and historical survey of European and American glass from the first half of the twentieth century make this a classic.

Ricci, Franco Maria. *Venini: Murano 1921.* Milan: FMR, 1989. This history of Venini is illustrated with gorgeous oversized color plates.

Ricke, Helmut & Ulrich Gronert. *Glas in Schweden 1915-1960.* Munich: Prestel-Verlag, 1986. The text includes 10 pages of information on signatures and dating pieces, and the illustrations are very good. (German text)

Ricke, Helmut & Lars Thor. *Swedish Glass Factories: Production Catalogues 1915-1960.* Munich: Prestel-Verlag: 1987. This reprinted collection of illustrated catalogs emphasizes Orrefors and Kosta and is excellent for identification. (German text)

St. Petersburg Museum of Fine Arts. *Murano Glass in the Twentieth Century.* St. Petersburg: Museum of Fine Arts, 1983. This exhibition catalog has good illustrations and is useful for identification.

Smithsonian Institution & Venini International. *Venini Glass.* Washington D.C.: Smithsonian, 1981. This catalog of a traveling exhibition has historical background, excellent chronology of Venini, a glossary, and good illustrations provided by Venini.

Sotheby's. *Arts Décoratifs Styles 1900 et 1925.* Monaco, Oct. 9, 1983.

Glass Since 1945: The Dan Klein Collection. London, Nov. 29, 1984. This was a pioneering collection and auction (139 lots) of fifties glass.

Arti Decorative del Sec. xx. Milan, June 7, 1990.

Venetian Glass 1910-1960. Geneva, Nov. 10, 1990. This beautifully illustrated hardbound auction catalog is also an informative reference.

Arti Decorative del Sec. xx. Milan, Dec. 13, 1990.

English & Continental Glass 1500-1960. London, March 25, 1991.

British Ceramics and Glass. London, Nov. 19, 1991 These Sotheby's catalogs, which include high quality photographs and information on fifties glass, provide excellent reference material for identification and study as well as market trends and price variations.

Stennett-Willson. *The Beauty of Modern Glass.* London: Studio, 1958. Written in the 50s, this well-illustrated book provides a good contemporary view of glass.

Warmus, William. *The Venetians: Modern Glass 1919-1990.* New York: Muriel Karasik, 1989. This small, beautifully illustrated catalog includes essays.

Price Guide

This, like other price guides, is just that — a guide. Prices fluctuate and vary from region to region, from country to country, and from time to time. Although the general direction of price change is usually up, there are cycles and instances of unusually high or low estimates. A determined collector paying an extraordinary price for a piece can inflate the market unrealistically. On the other hand, lack of interest or awareness of a collecting field, such as fifties glass, in geographic regions where modern decorative arts are not yet recognized, can present an equally unrealistic range on the low side. In addition, all price guides are short-lived, and as markets change, so the lists must be revised.

Fifties glass presents an added problem for compiling a price guide. As a collecting field, it is young, and although thousands of good pieces were produced, relatively few of these have yet come to market, and collectors are just beginning to show serious interest. The European markets are better established than in the United States, and in America, collectors on the West and East coasts generally show more awareness of good modern work than elsewhere. Statistical averages for prices are impossible, because the number of pieces that have come to market is small, and the prices have been changing rapidly. Since these objects are perishable, there is no way of telling how much of the glass has already been lost. It will take some time before we can determine the rarity or availability of specific series or models, and this will also influence prices.

Condition as a criterion for valuation should be obvious. Given similar pieces, the better the condition the greater will be the value. In the case of modern glass, this requirement is critical. Since it was produced so recently, it should be perfect. Glass in general is less forgiving than other materials which can be restored, such as ceramics, that can more easily absorb minor imperfections, or furniture, which is expected to have a patina and show some wear. Signs of use which are interpreted as charming on many antiques are disliked by glass collectors, and fifties glass should look quite new.

This newness might prompt the question of fakes or reproductions, and indeed, new versions of old styles have always been honestly made, particularly in Murano. In fact, Orrefors still produces a limited number of 40s and 50s designs and proudly identifies them as such. They are also very costly, because the level of skill required to make a new version is equal to that of the original, and few glassmakers have it. There has been, however, a flood of poorly made clowns and birds posing as earlier Murano pieces, and countries in the Orient have been turning out cheap imitations of other fifties glass as well. Reliance on signatures and labels or even on casual appearances is never enough. The collector must view and handle as many good examples as possible in order to develop an intuitive ability to judge quality and to identify other pieces.

The following list is from a combination of international auction estimates, auction sales, and antique dealer prices from shops and shows. It is only a guide and, of course, there can be no guarantee that similar pieces will realize similar prices, and the publisher cannot be responsible for any outcomes. As the field develops, the market will probably become less volatile and more predictable. As with other art markets, investment bears risk, but compared to other categories of art, the market for fifties glass is still undervalued. Ideally, the monetary factor will not overshadow the real value: artistic beauty, inventiveness, technical virtuosity, and a cultural legacy of a more innocent time.

To use this guide, the left hand number is the **page** number and the number immediately to the right is the **photo** number. The letters following it indicate the **position** of the item in the photograph: T=top, L=left, TL=top left, TC=top center, TR=top right, C=center, CL=center left, CR=center right, R=right, B=bottom, BL=bottom left, BC=bottom center, BR=bottom right. The right hand numbers are the estimated **price** ranges in U.S. dollars.

page/photo/position/price			
11	1.1		4,000-6,000
12	1.2	L	800-1.200
		TC& CR	1,200-1,800
		BC	400-800
		R	600-800
13	1.3		250-350 each
14	1.5		1,000-1,500
16	1.7		25-45 each
17	1.9		300-500 each
18	1.11		400-600
19	1.13		75-100 each
	1.14		75-100 each
20	1.15		250-350
	1.16		100-300
	1.17		100-200
21	1.18		100-250 each
	1.19		50-75 each
	1.20		50-75 each
22	1.21		100-200
	1.22		600-900
	1.23		100-200
23	1.24		100-200
	1.25		50-100 each
	1.26		150-300
24	1.27		150-300
	1.28		50-100
	1.29		100-200
	1.30		250-400
25	1.31		200-400
	1.32		300-500
	1.33		100-200
26	1.34		75-150
	1.35		50-100 each
	1.36		400-600
27	1.37		100-200
	1.38		400-600
28	1.39		2,500-4,000
29	1.40		2,500-3,500
30	1.41		4,000-6,000
31	1.42		250-350
32	1.43		200-300 each
33	1.45		75-150 each
34	1.47		150-300
	1.48		75-125
35	1.49		100-150
	1.50		100-150
36	1.51		50-75 each
	1.52		75-150
	1.53		75-150
37	1.54		100-150
	1.55	L	50-75
		R	75-125
	1.56		100-200
38	1.57		8,000-12,000
39	1.58	L	4,000-6,000
		C	7,000-9,000
		R	5,000-7,000
	1.59		350-500
41	1.60		8,000-12,000
42	1.61	L	3,000-5,000
		C	2,000-4,000
		R	3,000-5,000
43	1.62	L	2,000-4,000
		C	2,500-4,500
		R	2,000-4,000
44	1.63	L	2,000-4,000
		R	4,000-6,000
45	1.64	L	6,000-8,000
		C	4,000-6,000
		R	3,000-6,000

Page	No.		Price
46	1.65	L	8,000-12,000
		C	3,000-6,000
		R	3,000-6,000
47	1.66		10,000-15,000
48	1.69		2,000-3,000
49	1.70		200-400 pair
	1.72		75-125
	1.73		75-125
50	1.74		300-400
51	1.77		100-150
52	1.78		75-125
	1.79		60-90 each
53	1.81		100-200
	1.82		75-125
54	1.83		75-125
	1.84		50-100 each
	1.85		75-125
	1.86		50-100
55	1.87		50-100
	1.88		75-150
	1.89		50-100
	1.90		500-700 set
56	1.91		50-75
	1.92		50-75 each
	1.93		100-200
	1.94		50-100 set
57	1.95	L	50-75
		R	75-125
	1.96		40-60 each
	1.97		100-150
	1.98		75-150 each
58	1.99		200-400
59	1.101	L	6,000-8,000
		C	4,000-6,000
		R	4,000-6,000
60	1.102		3,500-5,500
61	1.103		6,000-8,000
62	1.104		5,000-7,000
63	1.105	L	4,000-6,000 set
		CL	8,000-10,000
		CR	12,000-16,000
		R	6,000-8,000
64	1.106	L	4,000-5,000
		C	2,000-3,000
		R	4,000-5,000
65	1.107		6,000-8,000
66	1.108		2,000-4,000
67	1.109		600-800
68	1.110		800-1,200
69	1.111		250-350 each
70	1.112		400-600
71	1.113		100-150
	1.114		50-100
72	1.115		250-350
	1.116		600-800 set
	1.117		75-150
73	1.118		7,000-9,000
74	1.119		100-200
	1.120		100-150
	1.121		50-75
75	1.122		100-150
	1.123		50-100
	1.124		50-75
76	1.125		75-125
	1.126		75-125 each
77	1.127		50-75
	1.128		75-125
	1.129		50-75
	1.130		40-60
78	1.131		1,000-1,500 each
79	1.132		250-450 pair
	1.133		50-100
80	1.134		50-100 each
	1.135		200-300
	1.136		150-200
81	1.137	L	2,000-3,000
		C	3,000-5,000
		R	2,000—3,000
82	1.138		4,000-6,000
83	1.139		4,000-6,000
84	1.140		1,500-3,500 each
85	1.141		2,000-3,000
86	1.144		7,000-9,000 pair
87	1.145	L	6,000-8,000
		C	5,000-7,000
		R	7,000-9,000
88	1.147		200-350
	1.148		300-500
89	1.149		600-800
	1.150		50-100 each
90	1.151		100-150 each
	1.152		300-400
91	1.153		75-100
	1.154		100-200
	1.155		75-125
92	1.156	L	5,000-7,000
		R	5,000-7,000
93	1.157		7,000-10,000 pair
	1.159	L	75-125
		R	150-300
94	1.160	L	4,000-6,000
		R	2,000-3,000
95	1.161		700-2,000 each
96	1.162		700-2,000 each
97	1.163		700-900 pair
98	1.164		250-350
	1.165		300-400
99	1.166		1,500-2,000
100	1.167		600-800
101	1.168	L	200-300
		C	500-700
		R	300-400
102	1.170		300-400 pair
	1.171		50-100
103	1.172		100-150
	1.173		150-250
104	1.174		300-400 pair
	1.175		75-100
	1.176		50-75 each
105	1.177	L	75-125
		R	50-75
	1.178		40-80 each
106	1.179	L	50-75
		R	100-150
	1.180	L	100-150
		R	75-100
107	1.181		75-125
	1.182		5-10
108	1.183		700-900
109	1.184		250-350
	1.185		1,000-1,500
110	2.1		2,000-3,000
111	2.2		2,000-3,000
112	2.4		1,500-2,000
	2.5		800-1.200
113	2.7		300-500
114	2.8		1,000-2,000 each
115	2.9		1,000-2,000 each
116	2.10		2,000-4,000
	2.11		2,000-3,000
117	2.12		300-500
118	2.13		500-700
119	2.14	L	600-800
		R	300-400
120	2.15		600-800
	2.16		300-400
	2.17		200-350
121	2.18		150-250 each
	2.19		75-100
	2.20		200-300
122	2.21		100-150 each
	2.22		300-400
123	2.23		300-400
	2.24		150-250
124	2.25		150-250
	2.26		400-600
125	2.27		100-200
	2.28		150-250
126	2.29		200-300
	2.30		100-200
	2.31		300-600
127	2.32		200-250
	2.33		vase 200-250 dish 100-150
128	2.34		400-600
	2.35		300-500
	2.36		100-200
129	2.37		250-350
	2.38		100-150
	2.39		100-150
130	2.40		300-500
131	2.41		250-400
	2.42		300-500
	2.43		250-400
132	2.44		200-300 pair
	2.45		150-300
133	2.46		100-150
	2.47		100-150
137	3.5		100-250
138	3.6		50-75
	3.7		75-125
139	3.8		50-100
	3.9		15-25 each
140	3.10		800-1,200
	3.11		100-150 each
141	3.12	L	150-200
		C	350-450
		R	150-250
	3.13		300-400
	3.14		250-450 pair
142	3.15		150-250
	3.16		100-200
143	3.17		250-400
	3.18		50-100 each
144	3.19		600-800
	3.20		400-600
145	3.21		40-60 each
	3.22		30-50 each
146	3.23		vase 25-50 bowl 20-30
	3.24		50-80 each
	3.25		4-8 each

Index

Illustrations are indicated in **bold**.